THE COLVER LECTURES
IN BROWN UNIVERSITY

1929

WHEN THE WEST IS GONE

By
FREDERIC L. PAXSON

COLVER LECTURES

HUMAN LIFE AS THE BIOLOGIST SEES IT
By Vernon Kellogg

THE RISE OF UNIVERSITIES
By Charles H. Haskins

THE NATURE OF LIFE
By W. J. V. Osterhout

AMERICA AND WORLD PEACE
By Honorable John H. Clarke

TYPES OF SOCIETY IN MEDIEVAL LITERATURE
By Frederick Tupper

MYSTIC ITALY
By M. Rostovtzeff

BACKGROUND OF THE RUSSIAN REVOLUTION
By Baron Alexander Meyendorff

Published by
HENRY HOLT AND COMPANY, INC.

Brown University, The Colver Lectures, 1929

WHEN THE WEST IS GONE

By
FREDERIC L. PAXSON

PROFESSOR OF HISTORY IN
THE UNIVERSITY OF
WISCONSIN

NEW YORK

HENRY HOLT AND COMPANY

CONTENTS

The Colver lectureship is provided by a fund of $10,000 presented to Brown University by Mr. and Mrs. Jesse L. Rosenberger of Chicago in memory of Mrs. Rosenberger's father, Charles K. Colver of the class of 1842. The following sentences from the letter accompanying the gift explain the purposes of the foundation:—

"It is desired that, so far as possible, for these lectures only subjects of particular importance and lecturers eminent in scholarship or of other marked qualifications shall be chosen. It is desired that the lectures shall be distinctive and valuable contributions to human knowledge, known for their quality rather than their number. Income, or portions of income, not used for lectures may be used for the publication of any of the lectures deemed desirable to be so published."

Charles Kendrick Colver (1821–1896) was a graduate of Brown University of the class of 1842. The necrologist of the University wrote of him: "He was distinguished for his broad and accurate scholarship, his unswerving personal integrity, championship of truth, and obedience to God in his daily life. He was severely simple and unworldly in character."

1916

The American Conception of Liberty and Government, by FRANK JOHNSON GOODNOW, LL.D., President of Johns Hopkins University.

1917

Medical Research and Human Welfare, by W. W. KEEN, M.D., LL.D. (Brown), Emeritus Professor of Surgery, Jefferson Medical College, Philadelphia.

1918

The Responsible State; A Reëxamination of Fundamental Political Doctrines in the Light of World War and the Menace of Anarchism, by FRANKLIN HENRY GIDDINGS, LL.D., Professor of Sociology and the History of Civilization in Columbia University; sometime Professor of Political Science in Bryn Mawr College.

1919

Democracy: Discipline. Peace, by WILLIAM ROSCOE THAYER.

1920

Plymouth and the Pilgrims, by ARTHUR LORD.

1921

Human Life as the Biologist Sees It, by VERNON KELLOGG, ScD., LL.D., Secretary National Research Council; sometime Professor in Stanford University.

1922

The Nature of Life, by W. J. V. OSTERHOUT, Professor of Botany, Harvard University.

1923

The Rise of Universities, by CHARLES H. HASKINS, Ph.D., LL.D., Litt.D., Gurney Professor of History and Political Science, in Harvard University.

1924

Criminal Justice in America, by ROSCOE POUND, Ph.D., LL.M., LL.D., D.C.L., Carter Professor of General Jurisprudence and Dean of the Faculty of Law in Harvard University.

1925

America and World Peace, by HONORABLE JOHN H. CLARKE, former Justice of the Supreme Court of the United States.

1926

Types of Society in Medieval Literature, by FREDERICK TUPPER, Ph.D., L.H.D., Professor of the English Language and Literature, University of Vermont.

1927

Mystic Italy, by M. ROSTOVTZEFF, Professor of Ancient History, Yale University.

1928

Background of the Russian Revolution, by BARON ALEXANDER MEYENDORFF, Reader in Russian Laws, Institutions, and Economics in the University of London (sometime member of the Russian State Duma, Senator under the Provisional Government, member of the Constituent Assembly).

1929

When the West is Gone, by FREDERIC L. PAXSON, Professor of History in the University of Wisconsin.

WHEN THE WEST IS GONE

CHAPTER I

WHEN THE WEST WAS NEW

The historian is not a prophet, and has no business to act as though he were one. By the very nature of his task he is limited in his investigations to those occurrences of the past that have left a record. He may not pretend even that all history is his oyster, for he knows only too well that at many of the critical moments when the course of history has been deflected the record was never made, or has been tainted in transmission, or has been lost. From the moderate number of events for which evidence exists he may draw only such conclusions as the evidence may warrant. And if he be honest with himself he must have a profound suspicion of every systematic attempt to explain the whole of any civilization. It is only as he respects the limitations amid which he operates that he is entitled to credence even within his special field. And when he deliberately departs from his field and tries to pluck aside a corner of the impenetrable curtain that hides the future, he must know the futility of his task. Only the theologian, or the economist, or the social reformer

3

dares to foretell the future. But the same allurement that leads these to attempt to know the unknowable, operates upon every human mind. It may well be debated whether the historian comes to his task as scientist chiefly, or as craftsman; but that he is human is not open to debate. He knows that error and ignorance and preconception are the stumbling blocks of prophecy; but he knows also, as a great biologist has expressed it, that all the knowledge any human may possess about the future must be derived from his knowledge of the past.

And so I propose, hopefully as a human, but modestly as a historian, to face the tremendous questions of national character, of national influence, of national destiny; and to bring to a focus, as nearly as I may, those factors from our knowable past that appear to have made in American civilization a unique thing, that have endured in our land in spite of the distractions of an industrial civilization and the dilution deriving from an alien multitude, and that in our generation are changing or disappearing so rapidly as to emphasize the questions respecting destiny that every nation and every administration must face. No statesman, no nationalist, no social thinker can escape some responsibility for the destiny of his group. He must peer around the hangings of the curtain, or try to lift its corner. He must guess the courses of events; and when successful accept the rewards with as straight a face as though he had foretold them. He must accept defeat without admitting that after all his forecast was but a guess.

Around the world today parties and philosophies are everywhere facing the future with a more than normal self-consciousness. But in only three of the major nations are the forecasts torn loose from the moorings of a continuous past. In Russia a new centre of gravity is revealing itself, and is upsetting all the ancient balances. In Italy the guarantor of a new revelation is ordering the ebb and flow of democracy to accommodate themselves to the restrictions and ideals of his fascist mind. In the United States an old formative condition that, more than any other single thing, has made the nation what it is, is gone. There are no data from the past by which to forecast the course of soviet control and the dictatorship of a proletariat; or to estimate the permanence of the artificial equilibrium of fascism; nor can the American statesman foresee his course in a world of narrow neighbourhood and financial penetration. Until our moment here and now, the mainsprings of our action have been a safe remoteness, the open frontier, and the psychology of the debtor class. The Russian and Italian revolutions, by convulsion and coup d'état, changed the direction of those nations. Quite as emphatically, though without a creak in the machinery or a drop of blood, the closed frontier has brought to us a revolution in "our lives, our fortune, and our sacred honour."

The West has gone, and it behooves us to look into our household and to examine the estate, to peregrinate our boundaries and to gaze across them at the world outside. We have hitherto regarded life from a setting in which the implicit condition was the West that was. Ever it was there, exercising its influence upon our course. When it was new, it formed our character as a nation, giving to the world in the process a new race whose advent was not foreseen and whose very existence was not realized until its character was formed beyond repression or recall. It is not possible, I must repeat, to foretell the future; yet every act of every statesman must be based on some assumption. He must move into the future as though he understood it. If in the years to come he should forget, or should not know, that the background of our life has changed, he would lessen the usefulness to us of a position that is even yet strategic, and to the world of an inspiration that has not ceased to be authentic.

We shall need, as we prepare ourselves for

an examination of the zone within which our
future aims must operate, to consider questions
of internal concern and external complication.
No one has posed the former more clearly than
our recent and kindly French visitor, André
Siegfried, who has asked, in his *America Comes
of Age* (1926), whether the United States is to
continue fundamentally British in its outlook,
or to acquire a new vista influenced by its newer
alien strains; whether it is to continue in the
ideals of an agrarian community or to yield to
urbanism; whether it is to remain generally
protestant in its religious thought, or to find a
new equilibrium based upon a growing influence
of the Catholic church. For all of these questions of internal concern there is something of
an answer that will carry us back to the simplicity of our frontier past.

For our external complications, equally
searching questions may be set up; are we con-
stitutionally capable of operating safely in a
world of close contacts? are we spiritually ready
for a shading of the independence of our American nationality? can we as lenders avoid the
pitfalls of an imperialism that had no tempta-
tions so long as we were the borrowers? are we
bound, in adjusting ourselves to the requirements of industrial society and the machine age,
to become merely an additional nation of the

western world, or will the traits of the frontier remain as permanent characteristics to dominate lives that never lived the life, and to preserve for American society its novel aspect?

All of these questions are too big for final answer; yet all of them I shall hope to bring to your consideration. But before we reach them, and that we may have something of a common understanding as we consider them, it is necessary to view the West when it was new and to inquire what it was. When next we meet, it will be useful to consider why it was that the West survived, as Middle West, despite the forces continuously working for its assimilation and conversion. And at the last will come the opportunity to face the larger questions of what we shall be when the West is gone. It will not be necessary to review the whole gallant story of the frontier, human and inspiring as it is; but we shall take a glimpse of three generations, each opening with an event of momentous significance for Americans. In 1763, the English Government believed that it was safe and wise to restrain the westward march of the Americans; and a generation of revolution was opened that ended for our purposes when, with the admission of Ohio into the Union in 1803, a new type of imperialism had been bred upon our continent. In 1824, when Henry Clay laid

down the philosophy of his American System
in the debate upon a protective tariff, there
opened another generation in which the question
was whether the West could be swung to the industrialism of the East, or to the localism of the
planters' South; and this ended for our purposes
when two authentic western leaders, Lincoln and
Grant, coöperated in stating and maintaining a
fresh conception of American nationalism. The
last of our three generations shall begin when
Mark Hanna counted the votes in November
1896, and revealed the fact that the West had
lost its drive, and had for the first time failed to
bring about a national compliance with its frontier needs. And in this third generation we are
living now, still uncertain what the future shall
bring to us, but clear enough that it will be different from the past.

On October 7, 1763, the first generation that
we are to examine took its start. On that day
the seals were attached at Westminster to a
proclamation for the reconstruction of the
American colonial empire of England. The
French war was over. France had given up the
hopeless contest, and had agreed a few months
before to surrender the eastern half of Louisiana
and all of Canada to England. Spain was in no
condition longer to resist, and having lost Ha-
vana in the war was ready to buy it back with

Florida. The western half of Louisiana was not seriously coveted by either Spain or England; but France was through, and the province was assigned in the settlement to its western neighbour, Spain.

The war was over, and whether it would stay over was as yet behind the curtain. There was need for readjustment of the relations between the English Government and its empire overseas; particularly now that the latter had been increased by increments from France and Spain. It was not the first time, or the last, that finite men sought to reconstruct their world; and the orderly arrangement to which King George III now gave his royal approval was perhaps as wise as that to which the statesmen at Versailles gave their assent a decade since. The Proclamation of 1763 at least did not seek to punish anyone, and it guaranteed to the conquered minorities a degree of freedom and protection that was embarrassing to England before many years had passed.

The part of this Proclamation of 1763 with which we are now concerned is not the series of paragraphs that stated limits for the new crown colonies of East Florida, West Florida, and Quebec. It is rather that part in which the crown sought to preserve the peace. "It is just and reasonable," the Proclamation declared, "and essential to our interests, and the security of our colonies, that the . . . tribes of Indians . . . who live under our protection, should not be molested or disturbed. . . ." And to this end the governors of the three new provinces were directed not to pass patents for any lands beyond the limits of their respective governments; and the governors of the other plantations in America were similarly and peremptorily forbidden "for the present, and until our further pleasure be known, to grant warrant of survey, or pass patents for any lands beyond the heads or sources of any of the rivers which fall into the Atlantic Ocean from the west or north-west. . . ." From the standpoint of an orderly administration of the empire there was much to commend the establishment of the Proclamation Line along the Atlantic watershed as a limit to the immediate occupation of the West; but its spirit was so inconsistent with the habits and aspirations of the communities whose future was at stake, as to make it one of the great indications of the cross purpose and misconception that, in another twenty years, produced the United States of America. We must see what those colonials were who were to be driven by over-protection into independence.

These seaboard colonies that lay between the St. Croix River and the St. Mary's, between

New Brunswick and East Florida, were planted mostly in the seventeenth century, without a plan, without a prospect, and without a future.

Without a plan: for the wholesale drafts that kings of England made upon the map reveal by their extreme generosity the absence of any deliberate intent. Here was a shore line of a continent. No one had found anything of use along it; but miracles might happen. Almost anyone who wished a license, whether to prospect or to operate might hope to secure it whether he be a royal favorite or a religious maverick. And the grants, engrossed and drafted in ignorance of a continent, were inconsistent with themselves and with reason and geography as well. But inconsistency mattered little, for the king had given and the king could take away; or if he alone could not, his courts could annul a grant or determine its dimensions.

Without a prospect: for in none of the plantations was there a real reconnoissance in advance of lodgment. No one had measured the resources of the soil, beyond the common observation that fish swam thickly in the sea, and timber stood densely on the hills. With few exceptions the men and women who took their lives and futures in their hands, and made the perilous voyage across the Atlantic, felt themselves expelled from the old home rather than

attracted by the new. The Atlantic seaboard
became a social dump, upon which were cast the
misfits of the European order. Driven out by
religious quarrels, by hunger, by politics, by
unsatisfied ambition, the great majority were
so unhappy in Old England and her neighbours
that the hazards of the wilderness by relativity
became attractive. They were getting away
from what they could not stand and took the
risk. It does not change the picture greatly
that some of them had visions of a happier
world, of success and satisfactions; or that most
of them sought in the new world for signs of
natural resources that might lead to wealth.

It was an unplanned trek that transferred
the life of Britain to the seaboard of America.
And it is one of the great paradoxes of our history that the chief of our sources of strength lay
in the general absence of resources worth exploiting. The colonies were no place for loafers
or for parasites. They provided homes for
men and women who worked for what they got.
They failed to rise to lofty elevations, but they
were founded so closely upon the ground that
they could not fall.

Without a future: for they already knew that
on either flank of the plantations a continental
neighbour stood entrenched. Spain's penetration
had worked its way around the Gulf of Mexico,

and had established outposts on the Florida
shore that placed a southern limit to any British
hope. France had visited the St. Lawrence, and
had pre-empted the drainage basin of the upper
lakes. Here was a northern boundary stake that
might not well be passed. And as for the
West:—the royal grants spoke grandly of the
continent from sea to sea, but neither the scribes
who penned the words, nor the kings who allowed them, nor the adventurers who sought
them, knew with accuracy what there was beyond
the rivers that drained into the Atlantic. They
might have suspected but they could not know
that the inland rights that Spain might easily
demand because of her occupation of the Gulf,
and those of which France was certain because
of her ownership of the St. Lawrence, inter-
locked in the middle of the continent and made
an articulated barrier against any reasonable
hope of British penetration. Not until all of
the seaboard colonies but Georgia had been
erected was the barren nature of the sea-to-sea
grants revealed, or was it proved that the question of the ownership of the interior was as yet
one for settlement by Spain and France alone.
LaSalle dropped down the Mississippi to the
Gulf at the very moment when William Penn
was launching his "holy experiment" in government. And a generation even after this Gover-

nor Alexander Spottswood rode across the Blue
Ridge into the Shenandoah (1716), hopeful
that he might discover some new route into the
interior of the continent. His Knights of the
Golden Horseshoe made much of the fact that
he and they had crossed the mountains; but it
was not their method that was to find a key to
the hinterland, or to discover the technique
whereby Virginia and her neighbours were to
challenge the Latins and penetrate our West.
To Spottswood, who wrote the Lords of Trade
about it, . . . "the long Chain of Mountains
w'ch run from the back of North Carolina as
far as New York," were a natural defence to
the plantations from Latin attack. His pro-
posals to cross the barrier and plant outposts
beyond it were not for the purpose of occupying
the interior or challenging the rival; but for
the strategic reason that thereby the approaches
to the bulwark of England's American possessions might be held.

There have been many Wests. At every
moment of American experience from the
first footholds until, a generation ago, the
railroads crossed the Rockies and ate up the
high plains, there has been a different West
at which Americans have gazed, and from
which they have derived more than a fair
share of all their problems. But the first

important West, that was American made, and that was not chiefly the result of direct immigration from Europe, and that may be looked at and studied against a background of an older American civilization, is the West that planted itself along the barrier that Spottswood desired to defend. About the time when George Washington was born the tide began to flow up towards the breaks in the eastern front of the mountain barrier, where the Susquehanna and the Potomac emerge on their journey to the sea. Here were the gateways through which poured for the rest of the century the raw materials for a buffer state. Quite as really as the eastern marches of Europe or the northern counties of Britain formed themselves into palatinates that were to defend the homeland from the invader, the barrier communities of the Appalachian valleys thrust the Indian away and forbade a penetration further east to Spain and France. The topography of the region gave it a different outlook from that of the seaboard settlements. These, on the seaboard, were separatist patches of life along the line of tidewater. They were founded separately, and lived each to itself. British policy encouraged each to look directly to England as parent and the source of all supplies. Inter-colonial trade was frowned on, and forbidden; and had the edict

of the crown been insufficient for this, the lack
of roads and the natural obstructions at the
river mouths would still have made it easier for
Charleston or Philadelphia to get to Boston by
way of London, than by way of a land trip up
the seacoast. When the time came for the first
through route on land to take its shape, the
route swung west from Philadelphia to the gaps
at Harpers Ferry or at Harrisburg, traversed
the valley system to the south, and returned to
the coast near the headwaters of the Savannah.
No road along the coast from Maine to Georgia
was of any consequence until independence was
an achievement long attained.

But in the mountain valleys the natural
courses ran parallel, northeast to southwest.
From the region of Albany to that of Chat-
tanooga access was, if not easy, at least possible.
And once the skirmish line of cabins began to
climb the Juniata and the Shenandoah a new
American community was born, stretching
across the western end of several of the eastern
colonies, but knowing no authentic lines of demarcation at any spot between the Mohawk and
the Tennessee. Colonial jurisdictions were tech-
nical at best for the mountaineers; and the simi-
lar problems of Indian removal, land acquisition, family establishment, and local government
gave them so much in common that a point of

view grounded in the soil and uniform along the west was born.

It made little difference from which of the seaboard establishments the farmer came. Few, of necessity, came out of New England; but from New York, and Pennsylvania, Virginia, Maryland, and the Carolinas, they were blended regardless of the basic stock. The new, and last, province of Georgia, planted in 1732 at the moment when this wave began to pour, was nearly as much the arrow head at the southern terminus of the valley system as it was the southern extremity of the seaboard line.

The palatinate idea was closely tied into the population shift. The proponents of the Georgia colony thought and talked of the dangers from Spanish Florida that threatened the Carolinas, and it seemed to them a humane move to shove the bodies of dependent and useless debtors into the post of hazard. Thereby they could kill two birds at once; gratify the growing spirit of humanitarianism as to the debtors and save the scalps of valuable members of society living in Charleston and points around it. Other of the less desirable elements of society, as the early eighteenth century rated them, were thrust into other posts of useful danger, in addition to those who were planted in the border mark of Georgia. From the Palatinate they

came, and from Ulster. In northern Ireland,
the Scots with whom England had sought to restrain and dominate the rebellious Celts, were
many of them weary of the task. They in their
Presbyterian congregations were ready for an
emigration; and the ship masters carried them
in wholesale cargoes to Boston, New York and
Philadelphia. The Penns sold them farms along
the Susquehanna and its branches to make the
eastern counties safe for Quakers; Virginia
granted farms to the Ulstermen, who figure in
our story as Scotch-Irish, in the Shenandoah
and beyond. New York received the Germans
and colonized them between the Albany outposts
and the scalping knives of the Five Nations, and
frankly conceded that a German who made a
farm upon the new frontier served society in
more ways than one.

The element of common and genuine hazard
was a powerful bond among the frontier groups
of the Appalachian valleys, to act as a tight
cement among the other common purposes. At
its side grew an equally binding feeling of re-
sentment directed at the parent colonies whose
ignorance, indifference to the frontier hazard,
and selfish exploitation of the provinces to their
own advantage, were a cankering exasperation
to the farmers of the West. By the time that
France had hurled its defiance to England by a

new attempt to hold the line of Lake Erie and the Ohio, the West was looking hither for more than the outposts of Governor Spottswood. Virginia gentlemen had formed a land company to speculate in Ohio Valley real estate, and homes rather than garrisons were preparing to establish an English frontier against the French. The fifteen years of war that followed the peace of Aix-la-Chapelle in 1748, saw England stretch herself to hold America; and saw in the cabins of the border a fighting front that could not be dislodged by any power France could mobilize. While the wars went on, the cabins moved as well. Braddock and Forbes cut their way across the valleys to the western outlets. The settlements ascended the eastern slopes, and without pause drifted down the western to the basins of the Ohio, the Cumberland, the Tennessee. And English thought, that had been cognizant of the new West as a defence of empire, failed to discover in it also a force of occupation.

The conquest of the Mississippi Valley was already inevitable before France gave up the fight and split her Louisiana among her conquerors. And English wisdom, such as the Lords of Trade possessed and the King in Council ratified, was blind to the power of spontaneous generation that the English frontier in America was showing. In the Proclamation of

1763, the line of prohibition, that forbade the further grant of lands west of the rivers flowing east, was obsolete before the order passed the seals. It was no more possible to check, or even to direct, the course of the American frontier than to stop a glacier, or to make the tides recede.

The West, this West, that was shaping itself behind the thirteen colonies, with a uniformity of back-ground and a unity of purpose that the parent colonies could not understand, attained a sort of fulfillment in the forty years that followed 1763. It is impossible to understand the inevitableness with which an American frontier had made Americans out of Englishmen; it is equally impossible to understand the measures of the Revolution, the forces that erected the Government of the United States, and the second revolution that set Jeffersonian democracy in the saddle for a generation, without a comprehension of the inability of the thirteen States to talk the same language with their offspring of the border. When this West took shape we first come upon an American set-up with a West against its East. We are even today not yet through with the antitheses between the East and West. But from first to last the Easts, like Britain, have ignored their Wests, and have failed to sympathize. And the Wests of every decade, like the colonials of 1776, have resented indifference, diabolized the absentee, and presented with driving and uncontrovertible insistence whatever point of view has for the moment been on top. It was on the English frontier, washed by tidewater in the seventeenth century, that the American was made; upon the American frontiers of the century and a quarter after the definition of the Proclamation Line, the consistent influence of the West was to keep the American character true to type, and to resist the encroachments of alien cultures, exploitative society, and industrial revolution.

This Old West, or New West, according to the direction from which it is approached, whose nature England so completely misunderstood in 1763, was in ten years or so pushing the fingers of its penetration along the Youghiogheny and the Monongahela, down the Kanawha and the Tennessee, and through the Cumberland Gap into the margins of the Kentucky blue grass. The elder statesmen of the East could not believe that England had meant the Proclamation Line to be a reality or a permanence, and were soon lobbying at London for new charters for new colonies west of the mountains. And the early comers in the Kentucky Valley were there in time to learn of the momentous events at Lexington, and to adopt the name for their cross-roads village.

In another decade or so, the western counties of North Carolina were in open secession from the eastern State, and demanding that the Congress recognize their right of self-determination, and admit them to the Confederation; and like their Virginia neighbours to the north they were wondering whether destiny with them was to be in connection with the seaboard republic or with a Mississippi Valley structure of their own.

In still another decade they were shouting tyranny at Washington and the Philadelphia Congress in language not unlike that of the eastern patriots who had been denouncing England; and Washington, triumphant rebel against England as he had been, was directing the military power of the young republic against rebels in his own New West.

And by the end of the century, less than forty years after England had foreseen the Appalachian divide as a boundary to settlement, a new political party, derivative from the western spirit though generalled by a Virginia planter, Thomas Jefferson, had settled the question of western rights by taking possession of the Government of the United States in the name of the younger settlements, and driving the Federalists into New England, on the road to oblivion.

Here along the mountain valleys was the heart of a West whose social driblets were oozing through the western mountain gaps into the margins of the Mississippi Valley, with an open continent ahead. What was this West, and why? How did it come about that the farmers of the border so often called the tune to which the United States must dance? There had been plenty of frontiers ahead of this. Rome, as she spread her conquests through Gaul to Britain and the north had seen recruits from Britain and Gaul and the other provinces, rise to direct the empire. But these frontiersmen of ours were farmers, whose essential acts were most commonly anonymous, and who were in fact the offspring of the East and the cousins of the rulers whom they sought to dominate.

The matter of definitions is of some consequence at this point, for the civilization of Europe did not come to America in a single leap; nor did that of the East, all of it, reach the West at once. The frontiers have been as numerous as their historians, and each of the students of the West has inclined to define frontier in the language of his own interest. Standing at any given point of vantage on the long road between western Pennsylvania and the Mississippi River, one might in less than half a century have seen the various precursors of civili-

zation pass by, each represented by a frontier
of its own. The correct definition to be applied
to any of these transitory borders depends
largely upon the momentary use to which the
frontier was being put by white men, or upon
its functional relationships as it has existed
with settled society behind it and primitive virgin soil ahead.

There was, first of all, the explorers' frontier, as the European invader brought one geographic region after another within the field
of recorded human knowledge. After this, or
sometimes parallel to it, came the frontier of
the missionary, the soldier, and the trapper,
upon which each of these scouts of society lived
his life. The first of them, the missionary,
worked upon the souls of the native inhabitants
who were destined to recede as the world became
aware of their existence. It is one of the mis-
fortunes of our history that all treatments of
the Indian side of our advancing frontier must
be chiefly unilateral. The native races, caught
in tragic situation by the cutting edge of a
harder civilization, were no more able to de-
scribe progress from the standpoint of the under
dog than were the men of Neanderthal, or the
cave-dwellers as they disappeared. A few rec-
ords scratched here and there, a few oral tradi-
tions, garbled in transmission, are all we have.

The whole history has been told by the prejudiced pen of the conqueror, and the true story of another of the junction points in the progress of society has escaped us. But the missionary, on his typical frontier, was a heroic figure, labouring to enlist the red man in the army of the Kingdom of God, whereas his contemporary, the soldier, was trying to attach the native to a different kind of empire, and was staking the claims of one great power or another in the new world.

The trapper, who began to ply his trade before the frontier of either the missionary or the soldier was fully explored, differed from both of his predecessors in that he, first among white men, lived on the land he found, and off it. He derived from its resources a basis of existence. My distinguished predecessor, Frederick Jackson Turner, made it clear a generation ago, that none of these advanced frontiers changed the face of nature, and that all of them gave way eventually when the frontier of the farmer made its appearance, and dotted the land with cabins and cleared fields.

The farmers' frontier, with which we at this moment have most concern, was no more the last of the frontiers than it was the first. There is a long succession of later frontiers that may be traced in American history as beside the farmer the miner, the lumberman, and the railroad plunged into the wilderness. Following them all came frontiers of established local government, of locally created capital, of industrial society, and of the various aspects of culture and religion. In every one of these fields the frontier affords a means of studying institutions while they are in the formative stage, and before they become inextricably involved in the complex of a going and sophisticated society. There are few of our social institutions that give to the student a fair chance to watch in repeated instances a fundamental process. Most events of history occur only once, and are scarcely recognized before they are past. We lack the ability to set up in a social laboratory an apparatus upon which we may follow the practice of experimental science, and control the environment in order to study a process. But on these various frontiers repetition under relatively uniform conditions is so frequent as to give us, for the fields of activity here at work, something more nearly approximating the laboratory method than we possess for most other matters of race, nationality, and institution. We might, if we chose, fix our attention upon any of the aspects of frontier advance; but for the study of the meaning of the West of the Appalachian Valleys it is the farmers' frontier that has the greatest significance.

This is our West, for the moment; and it may be approached with a variety of definitions. It was unquestionably a *region*. At any given moment, from the first plantations at tidewater until the last of the free land was gone, the frontier was the place where most of the inhabitants, for most of their time, were devoted to the primary tasks connected with the clearing of the soil, the first cropping of their farms, the erection of their cabins, and the establishing of their young families upon a basis of sufficiency. Its geographic direction from the older regions was generally west; and so we call it the West. But we call it thus, remembering that, at their period of beginning, Maine, Georgia, and Vermont were as much West as Ohio ever was; and that as the West swept over the continent leaving in its wake a cluster of social units in the place of primitive nature, the West of one generation became the settled society of the next. The New West became the Old West; and the Old West often ceased to be West at all.

But the West, or frontier, was a *process* as well as a region. As a process it relates to the growths that were taking place within the frontier region of the moment. Not only were homes and families getting themselves established, but social groups were forming, becoming self-conscious, and equipping themselves with such of the institutional outfit of the older regions as they could understand or desire. The survival values of the institutions of the colonies were being tested, and some of the institutions were being scrapped. As a process, the frontier was generally confined to a definable cycle. It began with the entry of the earliest cabineers upon a new region. It lasted while the generation of the founders cleared their farms and erected their homes. It ended when the farms had been developed into going establishments, when the farmer had neighbours across a party fence, when there were roads and county towns, and schools and churches, and when from the farm-house of the original cabineer the first of his children, born on this border, married and departed to work his destiny upon a frontier of his own.

The frontier is most often visualized as a *line* upon a map. Here its definition becomes less logical and more arbitrary. The line is drawn along the cleavage between organized society and the new social units whose process of creation is as yet incomplete. Since 1790 the decennial census has provided the basis for drawing such a line, and the statisticians of the census office, shading their maps to show varying densities in the population, have arbitrarily broken their zones of color at six to the square mile, at eighteen, and at forty-five. A line drawn across the map, just west of the margin of the area where the average population is six or over, runs through the heart of the region of the frontier. It indicates a cleavage that is as accurate as we need. When the first census was taken in 1790, this line ran not far from that of the Proclamation of 1763, where England had sought to halt the process of the frontier. On either side of it lay the region in which new creations, social and economic, were filling the mind of the people, and political expressions were revealing the necessities of frontier life.

The New West of the period of the Revolution, strung along the frontier line from Vermont, which became a State in 1791, to Tennessee, which became one in 1796, was a composite lacking the particularism and the parochial jealousies of the seaboard States. Its people came from most of them. It lacked the unblended Englishry of some of the older groups, for in its structure German and Scot had played a fundamental part. It had a topographic unity that brought its opinion towards a more definite focus, and it had a social uniformity that made its expressions of opinion more universal and forcible than those could be that were generated in the original States.

The influence of the frontier, as frontier, in producing this uniformity and shaping these opinions, calls for an examination.

There was a uniformity to start with. From the nature of the case, few persons sought the loneliness and hardships of a frontier for pleasure unalloyed. As the emigrants from Europe came to America generally because of a dissatisfaction so great as to obscure the risks and hazards of migration, so the westerner went west to better his condition. The rewards were so few and moderate, that if he had anything at home, wisdom bade him stay there and enjoy it. We may assume that he was poor. The man with ready money on an American frontier was an anomaly. From the start, the common poverty and the general expectation of better things, stamped upon the frontier population a greater degree of uniformity than ever prevailed in the communities from which the people came. It was a uniformity of those who have not; and further resemblances of age matched those of common poverty. The frontier was young. Among its members was a high proportion of young couples starting out from home. The aged and the dependent were as notably lacking from the procession west, as they have always been at Ellis Island or on the immigrant steamers of the new invasion.

Youth, poverty, and hope in an environment of grinding labor were the constituents of the frontier mind; and there have been few situations in which more has depended upon the physical and individual stamina of the man, and less upon the accidents of his possessions. Birth had little to do with success upon the border. It did not make the axe more sharp or the sod less tough. Education had little to do with it. Persistent physical labor was the lot of the able-bodied man or woman. There were few moments for intellectual relaxation; and although the wise and prudent lived longer than the foolish, the processes of establishment were the same for all. Wealth had less to do with success than in most society, for there were few stores in which to buy; few things to sell; and almost no labour to be hired. There were few uses for money that gave an advantage to the man who had it, where every man was working for himself, and where the labours of the pioneer filled every hour of daylight.

In a world of unusual equalities there developed readily an equalitarianism of thought. Upon the border there was a democracy of fact. Thomas Jefferson and the democratic leaders of the eighteenth century came to their democracy along the line of theory. Beginning with a philosophic equality at birth they advanced to a theory of democracy of *ought*: they were critics of the older world as they saw it, and believed that station and privilege were without justification. A world of equality *ought* to exist, to give every man his chance. Hence their democracy. But the frontier democracy was something of an inversion of this, though not less real. By observation the frontiersman saw that his neighbour was no better than himself; and he resented keenly the assumption by another of superiority. His democracy of *fact* made him resent the emergence of any privileged class, and made him restive under the thumb of any party, or local government, or nation that sought to impress itself upon his life without his full concurrence.

The New West of the Revolution could hardly have avoided political democracy as the expression of its equalitarian background. It stood, in its valley homes, among the mountains, in a sharp contrast to the world from which its people had been drawn. In the eastern States, communities were old enough for distinctions and rank to have appeared between man and man. In all of them, distinctions had been to some extent imported with the original immigration and the creation of a colonial nobility was often talked about. In the European world social class was everywhere a reality, and it was a rare man who had the strength and good luck to force the barriers between his class and the stratum above. Nowhere, either in the East or in western Europe, could one take for granted the democratic tendency that flourished from the moment the frontier cabins appeared on the edge of the American wilderness.

It is probably correct to say that the growing liberalism of the English colonies in America was the primary cause of American independence. The colonials had grown away from the customs and the classifications of the motherland, and no statesman had the genius to devise a new formula strong enough to close the gap and bring them back. But liberal as they were, there was now arising a still greater gap between themselves and the settlements across the mountains. The Americans had a degree of self-government in every colony, and were better off, and more kindly treated, than any other group of colonial subjects had ever been. But they resented absentee control and the misunderstanding that accompanied it. They had the franchise, and an electorate that voted for assembly members and local officers; but they had not reached a condition of liberalism that could dispense with a qualification of the right to vote. The godless were generally distrusted, and without church affiliation it was difficult to find one's way to polling places. They believed that ownership of property stabilized the citizen; and without property it was almost impossible to hold office, and hard to vote. The classes of seaboard society that had been educated in Europe, that ran the learned professions, that administered the church, and that spent the profits of commerce looked down upon the majority that tilled the fields. In some parts of the East the social system of England was having an imitation in America, as a country gentry grew up, whose gentility was separated by a wide chasm from the social roughness of the lower classes. America was more prone to democratic tendency than the England of its time; but the New West was so much more democratic than either that it was waiting for a leader to guide it to the promised land of political ascendency before the guns of revolution were silenced after Yorktown.

It was more than an extreme democracy, engendered by the uniformities of frontier experience, that made of the western a new type of American. There was, in the new region where he operated, a survival process whose tendencies were to accentuate those traits that made for aggressiveness, individuality, and an impatient habit of self-assertion. History knows little of the frontiersmen who failed. That they were many is too clear to doubt. The hardships of the pioneer life consumed the women and murdered the infants. In the old family graveyards that were nearly as numerous as the farms themselves, were buried the babies who were lost from lack of medical attention, from ignorance and prejudice, or from disease. The rapidity of population growth in the United States, which in our period increased the population something like thirty-five per cent in every decade, without much aid from immigration, is the more remarkable since it had to overcome an infant death-rate abnormal even in the eighteenth century.

And the mothers of the babies died as well. The position of the man at the head of a typical cabin-dwelling family was hard enough. He did the heavy work, he ran the out-door risks, he defended the frontier against the Indian; but his hazards were lighter than those of the woman whose interminable labours in the little cabin made her cook and seamstress, teacher and doctor; and with tragic regularity childbirth came, that she might enlarge the population of the tiny cemetery, and too often join it herself. The mature frontiersman, whose third or fourth wife lived long enough to be his widow, is a familiar figure in the family histories of the border; and

is much more numerous than the enduring
woman who survived as many husbands.

We know too little of the people of the West
who cracked under the strain, and died; too
little of those whose courage waned, and who
deserted the attempt at independence.   The
trails leading West were travelled by the failures
going home; but how numerous these were the
historian can only guess.

But those who survived became an heroic race.
In their youth they had made the great decision,
had cut free from the limits of home life, and
had risked their all upon an uncertain future.
With every step of the frontier process, they had
drawn upon ingenuity, resourcefulness, and
courage.   They took continual risks as the price
of mere existence.   They lived a life so remote
from contacts that it was easy for them to per-
suade themselves that they had done it all.   Government was far away.   With their own resources they had risked and won.   The western
who faced the survival process, and conquered
it, felt himself not only a democrat, but a self-
made man.   He acquired confidence in himself,
and a touch of that un-teachableness that some
observers have fancied to be a leading trait in
our American character.   As democrat he resented alleged superiorities; as an aggressive
and effective character, he trusted his judgment

and was restive under criticism or control. The urbanity that sometimes comes to men whose social standing is beyond dispute was rare on the frontier where social leaders had themselves made the platforms of their elevation.

There was a democracy. There was an intense individuation. More than this, there was something of a mental strain that filled the West with a race of minor poets.

No great poet rose from the American environment during the period that we are here considering, but the minor poets of the West were legion. They rarely wrote in verse; and many of them were indifferent even in their prose. Yet their minds dwelt in a world of make-believe that they often lived to see translated into reality. In older societies men were born to their station, and remained there until death claimed them. For many centuries there had been little change in life. Europe had been possessed, its fields surveyed and cropped, its vantage points occupied by favored classes, for generations before the American pioneers broke for the wilderness with cheap land beneath them and the world ahead. For these Americans the present was but a way station to the future, and to have regarded present conditions as permanent would have been to admit failure. It took a high courage to make the break at all.

As the pioneer trudged ahead of his little procession, along the rugged trails that pierced the mountain gaps, he was only incidentally living in his present. The future filled his mind; a future beginning with the rough shack that must shelter him for his first season; but a future of field after field of fertile land, of houses and live stock, of growing family and the education and religion that it needed. He carried debts upon his shoulders, but his inspiration was that of independence and a standing in society. In all the societies of which he knew or thought he knew anything, most social standing was an outgrowth of ownership of the soil. Here was the soil.

He expected to grow in opportunity and in dignity, and he did. The notion of progress, at which sophisticated societies often smile, and at which learned historians of antiquity can only scoff, came readily into the pioneer mind; and the American has not yet shaken it off. As he dwelt upon it, and tried to forecast the future that he might himself enjoy, or that his state or nation might experience, there developed the poetic streak that was a consistent inspiration. Sometimes he was King Arthur, sometimes Don Quixote; but he was ever something of a poet.

Here in our New West was the cutting edge of the United States as it fronted the untouched wilderness. It bound the rear of all the thirteen

States, and from them drew its people and its strength. It had a uniformity that our colonial period had never known. It was shaped by its environment towards democracy, towards an individual enhancement that raised the level of the common man, towards an openness of mind that looked upon change and progress as normal and upon a crystallized society as one diseased. Its pressure was ever in the direction suggested by the dominant traits that it could never avoid; and in forty years after the Proclamation Line it had captured the Government whose policies it had greatly helped to shape.

It has been necessary for historians to restate the whole of American history within the last generation, for once the notion of the significance of the pressures emanating from the open frontier has been appreciated a new meaning has appeared that transforms the American story. In the few minutes that remain, I wish to call attention to only one of the many newer views that the significance of the frontier suggests.

The American frontier presents a paradox in imperialism. It mutilated an English empire and turned it toward a process of slow disintegration; but it made an American empire upon which the effect of years has been that of intenser nationality and closer union. The colonies that remained to England after the American secession, and those planted since, have in many cases acquired for themselves that complete autonomy that the Americans desired. Their success has turned the British Empire into a Commonwealth of Nations, whose components regard themselves as entirely independent. The colonies that the American Republic has planted in the West, thirty or more, have all shared the common traits of democracy, individuality, and restiveness; but they have strengthened a federation, if indeed they did not give it an excuse for life; and they have been the provocatives of a nationality that today is one of the matters that we shall have to inquire into later, when the frontier is gone.

The new type of empire whose creation was on this frontier is a product of a frontier trait. It owes, indeed, one element to England; whose rulers wrote into the ancient charters that the colonials overseas should nevertheless retain the rights of Englishmen. This gave to English colonies at the start a difference from other colonies of other countries; and provided migrant Americans with an idea that never could be shaken off. But one need not read long or deeply in the literature of the eighteenth century to learn that it was simpler for the migrant to believe that he continued entitled to all his civic rights than for the older States to recognize that they must share equality with upstart commonwealths.

Yet the frontier pressure was continuous until the new-type empire was a fact. At the moment of independence there arose the problem of the public conquests. Armenia and Palestine, and the German colonies of eastern Africa were no harder problem for the allies at Versailles ten years ago, than were the western lands of the crown, included within the treaty limits of the United States but lying west of the proscription of the Proclamation Line, conquered by a common effort, and uncertain as to their proper ascription to any of the States. Herbert Baxter Adams began his long period of productive work at Johns Hopkins University some forty years ago by showing how the existence of any federation in America was conditioned on the treatment of these western lands, that underlay our New West. The solution of jealousies among the States, that made unanimous acceptance of the Confederation possible, was the transfer of western lands to the Congress, to be held in trust for all the people. Congress, in asking for this treatment, launched a policy in which it agreed that upon these lands new commonwealths should be created. And it had pledged a faith that was not its to pledge, that in due

course the new commonwealths should become
participants in the privilege and advantage of
the Union. Only by accident did the West avoid
a dependent status; only by self-denial did the
East refrain from maintaining a permanent
hegemony of law.

The first three States that were admitted to
the Union under the Constitution were in a sense
a test of the good faith with which the pledge of
equal membership was to be complied with. Vermont, Kentucky, Tennessee, were continued business from the days of the Revolution, and all
had real existence when England agreed to independence. They might have been admitted to
the revolutionary union, or to the Confederation, had the timid Congress not feared to add
to its perplexities by provoking quarrels with
the older States to which the three were off-
shoot. The sensitiveness of the older States,
who knew something of the British tendency to
countermand the charters, and to bestow on one
what had been given to another, brought into
the Federal Constitution of 1787 a guarantee
that no new State should be made out of an
older one without the older one's consent. And
when, while Washington was President, New
York assented to Vermont, Virginia to Kentucky
and North Carolina to Tennessee, and the number of member States was raised by three, there

was partial confirmation of the pledge of a participating empire. The States came in, they quickly forgot their period of probation and the federal Union grew in strength and dignity with each new increment of empire. But it must not be forgotten that it was a new sort of empire, for the ancient empires of the world and the contemporary monarchies had done and were doing business on the basis of superiority and force.

But the admission of Vermont, Kentucky and Tennessee was less than a complete assurance that the pledge was real; for in none of these was the public domain of consequence, and all their lands had been possessed by citizens, or pledged to them before their parent States assented. North of the Ohio came the first full test. Here, in the Northwest Territory, Congress had exercised control at every stage of the creative process. These were lands that various eastern States surrendered as the price of peace and union. Here Congress treated with the Indians and bought their lands. Here the surveys were directed and the lands were sold. In good time, as Congress had promised here was erected provisional government; and in more good time the popular element was admitted to it. And here, in 1802, for the first time, Congress authorized the creation of a participating State on land wrenched from the wilderness

which it had watched and cherished.   Forty
years after England forbade further extension
beyond the mountains, Ohio became a State.
The new principle of empire was a fact.   And
Thomas Jefferson, who signed the statute that
enabled, and the later statute that admitted, was
in his political relations living proof of the creative capacity of the frontier point of view, and
the pervasiveness of its influence.   A new dignity
for the common man, an enlarged influence, an
enthronement of an ideal of progress, and a new
conception of federal imperialism had been impressed by this New West upon the nation.

CHAPTER II

THE MIDDLE WEST

THE New West, which was new at the moment of the American Revolution, was new as a West in contrast to the older and more complex communities of the seaboard settlements; it was new also in the sense that its units were freshly born groupings thrown out or extracted from the life of the original plantations. It was followed by other Wests as long as there were fresh worlds for Wests to conquer. In the first generation it was a West of the Appalachian Valleys and it straddled the approaches to the interior of our continent. It continued to grow, without much change in method or result, for more than half a century after the generation of the Revolutionary West was over.

That first West had served to standardize the American race, for there were few infusions of alien blood for many years after the Proclamation of 1763. It served to democratize the American character to a permanent pattern. Our friends in biological science are strongly disposed to doubt the permanence of acquired characteristics; but in this angle of our social science it does appear that the social and political traits engendered by exposure to the American frontier were able to survive through many generations. This West brought persistent pressure upon the separatist States of the early Union, inducing them to moderate their pretensions to imperial standing, and advancing if not inventing in the United States a new model of imperial grouping with a balance between autonomy and centralization that has as yet not been improved upon. Its character as West persevered through the experiences of the Appalachian passes, the approaches to the Ohio country, the occupation of the Mississippi Valley, and the invasion of the basin of the Great Lakes. Its newer margins were forever repeating creations, re-examining the bases of social life, discarding the obsolete in law and custom, and giving to American institutions a validity independent of authority because they were founded upon repeated and independent selection and adoption. In the generation of the Revolution there was produced a clear American antithesis of East and West. In the next generation, that beheld the Great Migration and the development of the Ohio and Mississippi Valleys, the antithesis was the same.

But when half a century later James Bryce studied the States and described them with

friendly and illuminating pen, he saw and pic-
tured not two sections, but four; and André
Siegfried today finds the same four, each with
its special traits and point of view. The East
had been differentiated from the American type
before it was realized that there was a West.
Then came the South; and after it a farther
West, in which were curiously mixed the roughness and romanticism of Bret Harte and Mark
Twain, the corporate tendencies of the Southern Pacific and Boulder Dam, and the international sophistication of Los Angeles and Holly-
wood. It is not the West; nor was it in Bryce's
day. It is not East or South. For want of
better name the Far West, in strictly geographic
implication, has been adopted. And what was
once the New West of the Revolution, all the
West there was in the Middle Period of the last
century, has become for Bryce and us the Middle
West.

The great generation of our first West began
in 1763, at the moment when the restriction of
settlement to the seaboard stands as a monu-
ment to the futility of prevision in human
affairs. The great generation of the Middle
West, in which the West was to become Middle,
and in which the clear two-section antithesis for
the United States was to disappear, began perhaps with Henry Clay. It may be dated, with-

out more inaccuracy than is always inherent in
dated periods, when Clay laid down the full
elaboration of the American System in the tariff
debates of 1824.   Here was a philosophy of
national life, shaped up by a statesman of the
American frontier, whose certain result was to
show that the oneness of that frontier had
ceased, and that a South, differentiating itself as
a new American section, was to bring about a
three-cornered contest for American ascendency.
The causes of that fight, why the Middle West
stayed West and why the South did not, and
how in the triangular controversy the West became arbiter of our destiny until slavery had
gone and the Union had been enthroned, give
us the clues for an understanding of the Middle
Period.   There is an even century between the
moment of England's decision, which would not
work, and which wrecked her empire; and Gettysburg and Vicksburg which stabilized the
American Union, made possible a new step in
the direction of human values, and settled the
balance with the Middle West on top.

Two waves of liberalism, rising in the West
and flowing over the East, had in turn established themselves before the Great Migration
began its thrust at the beginning of the War of
1812.   The Revolution itself, as we have seen,
was the first of these.   The triumph of Thomas

Jefferson was the second. And in each of the instances success was followed by that cooling-off of liberalism that seems to come when enthusiasts in opposition are given the responsibility of management, and when young men grow old. The Jeffersonians had discovered how much harder it is to cure the ills of a social order than it is to promise to cure them. Before Madison took over the political estate from Jefferson in 1809, there were young democrats who thought that the older were pretty old. It was a revolt of these younger leaders that drove Madison reluctantly into war with England. Before the decade of the war ended it was even more visible that new ideas indigenous to the border were failing of satisfaction at the hands of Congress and the Virginia dynasty.

The Great Migration becomes visible as an unusually active shifting of population about 1811. By 1816 the first of its political fruits was ripe for harvest. Indiana became a State that year, to be followed in five more years by five more States, as much grounded in frontier life as it was itself. Mississippi, Illinois, and Alabama followed in annual sequence. Maine and Missouri would have been ready for entry with Alabama, had not the new issue of slavery forced them to lag, so as to carry the annual admissions to 1821. Six new States thus came

in six consecutive years. This was a carrying
out of the American theory of empire with a ven-
geance. The new delegations in the Congress
brought fresh notes into the debates in Washington, from States that had never known independence, that took the Union for granted, and
that expected much from it.

In getting at the point of view of this frontier,
or at that of any of them, indeed, there are at
least three sets of elemental problems without
an understanding of which the whole cannot be
solved. These are those of the land, the credit,
and the market.

First in point of time, and first in point of
logic, was invariably the land. Without an
accessible farm, the cabineer could have no meaning. When the price of land was too high, the
freedom of entry was restricted. When too
much of the land had been forestalled by specu-
lators in advance, hard feelings were certain.
But whatever the set-up, if we may know the
land economics of a new region we are able to
appreciate the matrix into which the new community must fit.

Next to the land, in both time and logic,
come the ways and means whereby the migration is financed. There is an almost unworked
field for investigation in this matter of the private finance of the emigrant farmer. We know

that he was usually poor; so poor that he had
little opportunity in the region of his origin.
We know as well that it cost money to make a
farm, even in the prairie States where land was
cheap. Without being able to make a balance
sheet for the transaction, it is clear that to move
an impecunious pioneer to a new establishment
called for outlay under several heads. First was
the cost of outfit. The wagon, the farm tools,
the household implements, however simple they
were, when multiplied by the thousands that represent the number of families in the Great Migration, stand for a substantial investment that
someone must make. Next was the cost of
transport. Even when the journey was only
from one county to the next, there were food and
fodder and sometimes shelter that could not
come from nowhere. The cost of buying, or
making the first payment on the land, can be
more nearly figured; and it came next. There
were few regions of the West where it did not
cost more to break an acre, and put it to crop
than it did to buy it. Sometimes the cost of
breaking the sod was two or three times the Government price. In any event it was a real investment, which when added to the cost of
erecting a cabin or shack, and shelters for the
stock, made a fourth item of considerable magni-
tude that must have stood between many an am-

bitious farmer and the independence he coveted.
And last, or at least last for our purposes, was
the expense of maintenance for a crop year, or
even more.   It was rarely true that enough
ground could be cropped in the first season of
occupation to produce enough food for man and
beast.   Until the farm was supporting its occu-
pants, paying interest on the mortgage, and
meeting the taxes, it must live in part on capital already accumulated.   This must be com-
puted in arriving at the balance.

Since by every definition the typical member
of our great advance was without capital of his
own, it becomes apparent that the credit contracts that he was forced to make must have
shaped the early years of his struggle for independence, and may have induced habits of life
or thought that would long identify the region.
It was not a case of here and there a debtor.
This case was, like other conditions of the
frontier, broadly uniform; and whatever joys
or troubles prevailed at Huntsville or Mobile
were likely to be as typical of Edwardsville or
Indianapolis, or St. Louis.

First the problem of the land.   After this the
question of the credit.   Next, the conditions under which the farmer might hope for solvency
and emergence from the debtor class.

We are even today faced with the western

demand for agricultural relief, and no responsible leader in the Seventy-first Congress fails
to admit the seriousness of the farmers' surplus.
But we and they sometimes overlook the fact
that the frontier farmer has always had to seek
salvation through the marketing of his surplus,
and that the question of our moment was quite as
acute a hundred years ago. The historical question that was wavering in the balance when
Henry Clay came home from Ghent and took
up the task of making a national leader of
himself, was whether the border American was
to develop into another peasant farmer such
as the world had ever known; a farmer who
dragged a mere existence from his soil, and
owed service and dependence to his protecting
lord; or whether some means could be found
whereby the one thing that the farmer had to
sell, the produce of the soil, could be turned to a
profit that would pay his debts, leave him an
accumulation of capital, and set him free.

The old frontier of the Appalachians engendered, as we have seen, a generation of fiery in-
dividualists, impatient of restraint, jealous of
distinctions, and imbued with an equalitarianism
that the genius of Thomas Jefferson turned
into a new political party of which he was, and
is the prophet. The new West of the Great Migration continued to produce men of this spirit,

and the philosophy of Jefferson refused to die. But this Mississippi Valley West produced construction as well as equalitarianism. The constructive genius of the period of the Old West was at the Eastern and conservative end of the table, in Alexander Hamilton, the Federalist; but the frontier that we have in view bred its own.

Henry Clay saw the depression that an unsold surplus created, saw the stake for the western farmer that was involved, and gradually pieced together the elements of the first national policy that was offered as such to the American people. He came to his task with all those traits that his frontier emphasized. To his high personal spirit was added a feeling of national humiliation that he had gained as he saw the United States trailing the European kite in the years of the Napoleonic wars. Dependent on the external world, and shaped by the necessities of the Europeans, he saw his country barred from self-sufficiency unless it should by its own effort create it. Out of the ever-present western farmers' surplus he conceived the need for a home market of consumers; out of the dependence upon the European manufacturer he adopted the idea of economic independence through a protective tariff. He saw that the industrial working class would eat the surplus; and that good roads and navigable streams would cut the costs of freight. His American System was a defiance of all the world, and a program for a national economic independence. It was founded on forethought, not on drift; and the place of each section of the United States was thought out in advance. It has provided, to a startling degree, the sailing directions for the United States for more than a hundred years.

But western in its inception though it was, and acceptable to the West, the American System never brought to Henry Clay the reward he coveted. It was Jackson who won the personal leadership of the West of the Great Migration. The emotional stresses of the frontier found little relief in the intellectualism involved in an appreciation of the American System. The western citizen agreed with Henry Clay, but his heart warmed up when he thought of the rival leader. Here was an Indian fighter, a general, a protector of his men against officialdom, a warm lover and a heavy hater—a personification of those intangibles that were the product of the soil. He was a martyr too, for his merits had been discounted by the eastern party leaders. He crowded the author of the American System out of the picture in the election of 1824, and four years later came triumphantly into Washington on the crest of the third of our series of

waves of western liberal opinion. He was rival
to Clay, but he was not a bad Clay man. The
principles for which Clay stood were accepted
by so many of Jackson's adherents that it is
clear that each of the pair was authentic personification of a part of the western mind and that,
while Clay commanded its intellect, Jackson inspired its soul.

It might well have been that Clay could have
won the high place to which he aspired had there
not been a flaw in his reasoning on the American
System that made it less universal than he
thought. The West, as West, liked it and voted
for it, as did the East; but a new set of causes
had begun to divert the interest of the South,
continued to divert it for a generation, and
brought to the political equilibrium the third
of our regional points of view.

The old classification of East and West began
to fail as soon as a southern crop appeared for
which there was a market.

We have gone a long way from the historical
interpretations of my youth, when Von Holst,
and Henry Wilson, and the New England aboli-
tionist historians ascribed the clash between
North and South to a kind of original sin that
made southern gentlemen like to hold their fel-
low men in slavery while their northern con-
temporaries were more permeable to the aspira-

tions of human freedom. We begin to see instead, an economic cause set loose by Whitney and his gin. We see and appreciate what had to happen to a world which had always shivered, and had always searched for textiles to keep its people warm, when a simple mechanical invention brought into the market an inexhaustible supply of a cheap fibre that could be easily worked into many varieties of useful cloth. When Henry Clay began the intellectual construction of his system, not long after his return from Ghent, the leaders of American thought were still of the old belief that slavery was a burden, and was in the course of ultimate extinction. They had not seen or weighed the meaning of the new market that provided the southern farmer with a positive profit wherever climate and soil made possible the raising of a cotton crop.

The cotton fields were already pushing out of Carolina and Georgia into Alabama and Mississippi. The slave, whose economic usefulness had been doubted, had found a job at which, in spite of his native indolence and his blunted aspirations, he could be made to produce a profit. The markets were clamoring for cotton, and still more cotton. Whatever it cost to raise it, it could still be sold. For three quarters of a century the demand was to continue, and saturation

was not to be reached or threatened until the
cotton belt had crossed the southern zone and
established the plantation upon the plains of
Texas. It was a universal and untouched market for cheap textiles that lifted part of the
southern population out of the hopelessness of
the western farmer, and led it from a repug-
nance to slavery to a grudging apology, and
from this to a devout admiration of slavery as
an institution given by God for the advantage of
white and black. Slavery, exclaimed Calhoun,
in his earlier frame of mind, "is an unnatural
state; a dark cloud which obscures half the
lustre of our free institutions!" But the later
Calhoun recanted his belief, and re-stated his
conclusion: "Many in the South," he said, "once
believed that it was a moral and political evil.
That folly and delusion are gone. We see it
now [1838] in its true light, and regard it as the
most safe and stable basis for free institutions
in the world." Clay could not foresee this revolution in southern thought; he scarcely recognized the deviation that was already at work
when he began to construct. He could not know
that he would live to see a South challenging
his West, and even the nation that he loved;
and steering a course whose destiny was separa-
tion, under influences that were brought into

existence the moment that it found a market
for its special crop.

In the debates of 1824 the historian can see
the beginnings of a recognition that for one reason or another the North and the South were
developing along different and divergent lines,
and that these lines were pushing into the West
to destroy its unities. Here is neither time nor
place to go into a prolonged analysis of the
financial ties, the social organization, or the
mental traits that came upon southern agriculture as it reorganized and grew under the pressure of an unsatisfied market. Labor there had
to be, and so the slave was used and the prosperous planter soon forgot that he had once imagined slavery to be a defect in a free social order.
But perhaps the recrudescence of slavery is
not the most important of the cotton consequences.

There were changes in the social organization
of the newer regions that broke the old uniformity of the West. The normal process had here-
tofore been one in which the cabineer, clearing
the land with his own hands, erecting his shelter, raising his family, was the type individual
during the frontier episode. As the frontier
passed into its second phase, with most of the
clearing done, and with the middle-aged pioneer
beginning to enjoy the fruits of his exhausting

labour, there was a normal period of a post-frontier, dominated by men who had been shaped by the pioneer hardships that were receding now into memory and were being idealized as they receded. There was increasing population, accumulation of wealth, the growth of towns, the erection of schools and colleges and churches. And the way was preparing for a new generation of agricultural society, with growing industrial permeations and increasing solvency.

But the southern cycle had a different orbit. It started, as did the northern cutting edge that advanced upon the forest, with the free cabineer, for rarely was the negro slave adaptable enough to be a useful agent in the processes of the pioneer. But in the period corresponding to the post-frontier on the northern border, the cotton planter was likely to appear upon the southern. His needs could not be met with single-family farms. He worked with slave gangs and overseers. His profits were related to management and a division of labor adapted to the mental habits of his blacks. In its second phase southern agriculture in the cotton country saw a lessening of white population, a multiplying of the black, and instead of a growth of towns and a spreading of the social net, a series of plantations making cotton, with here and there a planter's mansion or an overseer's home; and

clustered near them the squalid cabins of the
negro laborers. There was less free wealth than
a northern area accumulated in its post-frontier,
for the planter was ever under pressure to enlarge his fields until he became land-poor. And
he was forced in buying his labor to tie up elab-
orate capital that could not thereafter readily
flow with the markets. Instead of greater fluid-
ity of wealth, the trend of the plantation country was towards greater rigidity; until we may
doubt whether it was the negro who was slave
to his master, or the master who was the slave
of his economic order.

And in its third phase came the law of dimin-
ishing returns. Just as the northern zone was
passing from the psychology of the post-frontier into that of a prosperous agricultural zone,
with the local industrial supplies developing on
local capital, the planter South faced a decline
in crop yields. Single cropping had its sure
result in lessening the fertility of the soil that
was not too rich in the beginning; and manure
was scarce where herds were kept small by lack
of pasturage. The prudent farmer sold his
plantation, and moved on to fresh soil, leaving
his buyer to hold the basket. But the average
planter was as likely to begin to borrow, to live
on his mortgage, to die in debt, and to hand
over his estate to be broken up and operated by

the poor white farmers who perpetuated the hardships of the old frontier without the spirit and the hope that gave it life. The specious profits of the cotton crop; the agricultural organization that it entailed; the social order that it created; the financial network with which it bound the people; have perhaps more significance for the historian than the visible fact of slavery. But in any event the South was living in a new cycle, with a pace set by the planter gentry. It had its market, and its interest could not be attached to the marketing philosophies of Henry Clay. It shipped to a European buyer, and brought its merchandise back on the return trip; and it came to feel that the tariff so inherent in the theory of the American System, was merely a sectional steal to aid the North at southern cost. And thus it was that the emotional appeals of Andrew Jackson gave him southern votes, whereas the intellectual system of Henry Clay left the new South cold or worse.

In the generation that ends at Gettysburg and Vicksburg, the South ceased to be the West, and became enchained to a destiny of its own, in one of the great tragedies of social history. But the West stayed West. It was as West that it gave Clay his elements for constructive thought. It was equally as West that it produced that re-

vival of Jeffersonian equalitarianism that we
know as Jacksonian democracy. It created the
new majority of 1828, and kept its Democratic
Party dominant for a generation. And it was
still as West that, when the later Jacksonians
made and solidified their political alliance with
the South, the newer borders of the West produced another appeal to human rights, revolted
against slavery as the emblem of differentiation,
gave birth to the Kansas-Nebraska schism, and
brought into existence a new Republican Party.

The roots of Abraham Lincoln lie close to
the old West of the Appalachian Valley; but the
influences that shaped him were the tendencies
under which the children of the South moved
into the Northwest and continued in the belief
that slavery was in the course of ultimate extinction. Cotton was not a great crop in any
of the Border States. It was an impossible crop
in any of the Northwest States; and no other
crop was found in which slave labor could be
put to remunerative use, or for which an inexhaustible market could be discovered. The
northern section of the Mississippi Valley retained its ancient unifying qualities, its democratic trend, its idealism, its free initiative. It
continued to look to the nation as an entity
whose business it was to protect the individual
and give him opportunity. It demanded land

for its farmers, for its railroads, and for its schools and colleges. It perpetuated the kind of Americanism that was the typical Americanism of the period of the Revolution, and it continued to be the most American part of the United States. The South was a different section, with a different slant, and with a tragic trend. In the northern section of the West rose the new party that forced the issue, elaborated the idea of freedom, provided the leader, and by its economic and military weight maintained the Union.

While the West stayed true to the American standard in this generation after the launching of the American System, and while the South followed a new economy to destruction, the East fell under the influences of the industrial revolution that was changing the social map of Europe, and drew away from the old uniformities and parochial qualities of American life.

The old East, the East of the Revolution against which we first observed our West, was not so far removed from its past as to conceal the fact that it was once itself a West. Here was the frontier of Old England in a new world; and here crystallized the interests that England under the Georges could not comprehend. The seaboard towns had passed through their frontier phase long before the French wars were over. They had entered their own post-frontier and passed through it. They retained a restlessness under absentee control, a determination to go their own gait regardless of British influence, a habit of talking about freedom and what it meant, that look like survivals of their frontier days. But at the moment of the Revolution the East was in a course of adaptation whose natural results might have carried the Americans into a close resemblance to English society of the eighteenth century. The evolution of the country gentleman, the habits of the commercial class, the traits of the professions, continued in their approximation to English types well down towards the moment when the Jacksonians seized the reins of power in the name of democracy and the common man. In a way they preserved an English civilization after the parent was itself undergoing a transformation, much as the Middle West conserved the spirit of the old Americanism after that spirit had ceased to be universal in the United States.

The alterations that came to English life, and to all the life of western Europe, were based on steam and the rise of the manufactures, the concentration of capital in a managing class and the rise of an urban working class, and on the other phenomena that we have come

to associate with the industrial revolution. At
the moment when the Jacksonians were exult-
ing over their victory and the downfall of the
corrupt aristocratic classes of the East, the East
they thought they fought was obsolete, and was
on the verge of new developments to bring it into
line with the new life of modern Europe. For
the next half century, while the West conserved
the old Americanism, the two deviations of the
East and South brought new problems of balance into the American scene.

The introduction of manufactures, the rise of
urban society, and the injection of new alien
groups changed the direction of development
for the northern part of the eastern seaboard as
vitally as the appearance of a cotton market
changed that of the South. There is not much
continuity between the pre-industrial eastern
towns of the eighteenth century, and the industrial cities of the last half of the nineteenth. In
the former was produced a crystallization of the
social orders, and a series of distinctions between
man and man that revolted the citizen of the
frontier as long as he saw no chance of attach-
ment to the upper grades. But the towns and
cities were after all more or less a consolidation
of rural conditions. Many of the comfortable
estates were farmer-owned or farmer-derived.
The working people had cousins on the near-by

farms and thought of themselves more as farmer folk living in town than as proletarians of
a permanently inferior order. The industrious
apprentice had not lost the promise of Hogarth's
etchings, and the journeyman had as good a
chance of marrying his employer's daughter as
Benjamin Franklin, with his loaf under his
arm, had of crowning his long life by associa-
tion with kings.

The condition precedent to the rise of the
cotton planter class in the South was the mechanical invention that put cotton on the market. The condition precedent for the North,
was the acquisition of the free capital for industrial investment without which the factories
could not be built, and steam and the water
powers could not be harnessed in their service.
The European factor was ready enough to advance credit to the planter in order that the
flow of cotton bales might not be interrupted,
but he had no enthusiasm for a loan that might
bring forth in New England a textile establishment whose success would curtail the field
of his own operations in America. The capital to be used had to be accumulated at home.
Since the debtor condition of the American colonies had been chronic, and since few surplus-
producing industries were found in the United
States before the French Revolution, it requires

no argument to prove that manufactures in the
United States were forced to lag behind those
of England and western Europe. But the
French wars helped. The market for American bottoms, the trade in naval stores, the demand for food, the profits of neutral carrying,
the opening of the China trade and the whaling
industry all did their share in laying the foundations of our first non-agricultural fortunes.
And from these fortunes came the surplus that
sought hesitant adventure in the erection of factories even before the peace of Ghent. With the
rumble of the first factory begins the deviation
that soon made in the East a new civilization of
which the American of the West had no conception.

The steps by which industry turned the old
East into a section different from the West and
the type of American that the West conserved,
need only be suggested here. In the fifty years
after the tariff of 1816 the American working
class was born, and began to be class conscious.
The factory must have workers; the workers
could not own the plant. The profits of the
owning company depended upon a ready supply of labor, not too independent in its mind.
The longer the labor stayed on the job the less
it resembled the typical farmer of the frontier
tradition. Resourcefulness diminished, and

hope faded too. The rural regions of the East continued to furnish their increments of emigrants to the free lands of the West, but the city dwellers gave less than their share to the procession west; and more than their proportion of the pioneers who failed.

In another way the factory introduced new standards to the East. It bred large fortunes. It is an interesting fact that the earlier great fortunes of the United States, whose prudent investment probably saved the treasury from disaster in the war of 1812, were those of recent immigrants not yet fully absorbed into the native strains. John Jacob Astor, the German, Stephen Girard, the Frenchman, and David Parish, the Englishman, bought the national stocks when older Americans either had no cash, or kept it. But a crop of new fortunes, native to the soil, and derived from the profits of industry, made its appearance simultaneously with the enthronement of Andrew Jackson. The millionaire was as new a species in America as the working man; and in the early years he was as unconscious of his class character. However, the social classes drew away from each other as the years went on, and more and more the civilization of the East and North came to resemble that of the growing cities of modern Europe. The southern gentleman, when he

fared abroad, was aware of similarities that
made him feel at home among the English country gentry and the landed aristocrats of the
continent. He found that they, like him, looked
with some scorn upon the *nouveaux riches* of the
industrial revolutions.   Neither they nor he
could know that both were the outcroppings of
a civilization that was gone. Both were to lose
the position of vantage, the European as the
tide of proletarians increased; the southerner
before an alliance of the industrial with the type
American.

Industry, with its attendants of capital, labour, and the magnate, led the East away from
some of the simplicities of American life.   It
brought into being the city, and the city became
at once a generative power producing changes
of its own.

There was not much urban society in the
United States before the war of 1812.   The
residents of the cities, wealthy and sophisticated
as they might be, had still so much of country
in their blood that the city was only a trans-
planted and congested rural place; and a mile
or two from any city centre brought one to the
open fields. The town was not an organic body
with a social habit of its own. This was created when the factories on the outskirts brought
labourers to town, and these lodged in outworn

mansions, or in jerry-builders' cottages. The
towns grew in size. The family pump became a
source of pest. The cess-pool was a menace.
The very fact of neighbourhood and volume
meant a new organization that felt its way into
city government in the middle period of the
last century, and when the Astor fortune put
a part of its accumulation into the Astor House
on lower Broadway in 1836, we may say that
an urban period was fairly under way.

Not only did the cities grow, but they changed
as more and more of the inhabitants lived in
lodgings, not in homes; and needed to be en-
tertained and to be controlled as much against
the habits of their idle hours as against the wiles
of wicked parasites. From the mansions to the
tenements they presented a set of pictures new
upon the American scene. The re-casting of
municipal law that the cities made necessary is
not yet nearly complete. Their franchises provided new sources of wealth for those who could
control them, and gave a new meaning to the
politics of their control. The South escaped
almost entirely the consequences of city life.
The cities of the West remained rural concen-
trations for another generation until the industrial revolution was ready to press across
the mountains. The urban statesman and the
city politician were quite as much the contri-

bution of the change in industry to American
life as were any other of its phenomena.

And the statesmen and politicians found a
new source of strength, as well as conditions re-
quiring a new technique, in the fact that before
the urbanization had far advanced it ceased to
be American and became polyglot. The oppor-
tunities of American life which offered more to
the common man of Europe than he thought he
had at home, helped to induce the immigration
that began to pour in the fourth decade of the
last century. The accidents of Europe had
more than this to do with it.

It is of course a commonplace that Irish
famine induced an exodus. For the tenant
farmer, free land had always an attraction.
For the starving tenant farmer, America looked
like paradise. He came of his own volition.
He slaved to bring his sweetheart and his rela-
tives. He was sometimes sent; as amiable poor-
boards paid the charges of transportation for
their wards to the land of welcome and of plenty.
And in the growing American cities he did the
heavy work, joined his kind in gregarious
groups, learned that after all the millennium
had not come, and sought for friends. To the
urban politician, he meant so many votes, Tam-
many became his patron, and accommodating
legislators gave him the franchise before he had

got out of his system what Americans would like to believe were the toxins of the old world, or had adjusted himself to the aseptic purities of democratic life.

It is also a commonplace that the Germans came, driven by a combination of poverty and politics not yet fully analyzed. As their numbers grew, and as the Irish multiplied, we have the usual phenomenon of nativism to interpret; but we are here less concerned with this than with the consequences of the mixture to which the East was more openly exposed than either West or South. The new immigrants followed the usual channels of travel, and reached many parts of the United States. Oscar Straus has told how his father, a peddler with his wagon, established himself in Georgia, and raised a family of as sound Americans as we have possessed. Carl Schurz came with romantic background, and little else. His Americanization took less than a decade. In half that time he was speaking in public in an acquired language better than most of his contemporary statesmen could speak their own tongue. But none the less the immediate consequence of the immigration before the Civil War was to make a mixture in the East, which the South escaped, and of which most parts of the West knew little. Influenced by the alien groups, by the

urbanization of the centres of its life, and by
the spread of industry, the East was led from
its old standards towards a novel goal.   The
South was forced by plantation economics and
by the slavery statesmen into a different deviation.   And the native faith and life, so far as it
survived, lasted best in what was still the West.
The upper Ohio Valley, and the upper Mississippi carried on the tradition, escaping in large
measure the causes that elsewhere produced the
other two sections whose habitual rivalry gave to
the West an added meaning as the possessor of
a balance of power in American politics.

For most of this generation after Clay
launched his full-blown American System as a
sailing chart for the republic, the West remained the West; and there was nothing much
beyond it.   There was land, of course, and half
a continent.   But the best scientific opinion that
the Government could command had established
the fact that the frontier farm could never leave
the Mississippi banks far in its rear.   As the
slopes ascended from the Father of Waters to
the Rocky Mountains, the rainfall lessened, and
a desert barred the way.   The American Desert
was not nearly as real as it was imagined.   The
belief in it was, however, genuine, and its at-
tractions were so slight, its accessibility so difficult, that the Republican Party had been pro-

duced by its wave of western liberalism before any considerable encroachment upon the Indian lands of the high plains began. Oregon had been occupied and California taken, but the emigrants to either had passed cheerfully across the intervening plains without a desire to settle on the way. And with the so-called desert still a barrier, a new American region was appearing at the moment of the Civil War that was farther west than the West, and yet was neither East nor West nor South.

The Far West owed its sudden appearance on the map, and its spectacular entry into our national life, to a mixture of causes different from those that have ordinarily produced a new region and its group of States. Of course the pioneer farmer was there. In no section has he been absent. The Oregonians began to trek while Jackson was President. They occupied their Columbia Valley and laid the foundations for an eventual State before the war with Mexico. They would have overflowed in course of time, and certainly would have brought about an American penetration of California even had there been no Mexican war at all. But it was not the persistent pressure of the farmer that either made the Far West or gave to it its peculiar identity. It was rather the accident of gold, which spread the tentacles of a vast attraction in regions where the call of the frontier was not usually heard, and among classes for whom the thrills of independence in the single-family farm had no charms. The population of the mining camps had little in common with that of our typical farming frontier. Before the Civil War brought an end to the generation that we are now considering it had become necessary for common speech to recognize the new arrival, and to record its difference from what was tradition- ally the West. The term Pacific Slope was too narrow in its meaning, for the mining camps, started in California, spread not only up and down the coast, but in the decade of the Civil War they reached east across the divide of the continent. There were mines in Nevada and Arizona, in Idaho and Montana, in Utah, Col- orado, New Mexico and Wyoming. Here and there someone has called the region the mineral empire or the inland empire, but it is the term Far West that stuck. From the eastern margin of the mines to the Pacific, the Far West be- came a zone apart.

The special necessities of the mining camps, and their peculiar courses of development, con- stitute the first of the reasons for the deviation of this new section from the courses of the ancient order. Lacking the uniform constitu- ents of the old frontier there was lack of uniformity in the social and political output, and a social border separated the West of the Mississippi Valley, which now in self-defence comes to be described as the Middle West, from the Far West of the mining States.

In a second way, there was capital for investment in the mining States at an earlier period than in the Middle West. Only by years of good luck and painful industry could a farming frontier get itself ahead. But on the mineral frontier now and then someone struck it rich. For most of the men who sought their fortunes in the mines life was as hard and independence was quite as uncertain as for those who followed the unromantic plow; but the bonanza kings acquired unheralded fortunes, too big to be lost in dissipation, to be spread in glittering ornaments upon their wives, to be turned into the palaces in which they thought for the moment they wished to live.

They had local money to invest. If one could make a searching study of the Fair estate, tracing it from the moment of triumph when James G. Fair opened the tunnel into the chamber of the big bonanza, and could discover what Fair and his associates did with the hundred or more millions of dollars that they took out in profits from that gigantic pocket in the next half dozen years, the result would answer most of the queries as to why the Far West was not still West or even Middle West. It lacked the uniformity of origin, and it escaped the uniformity of resultant thought. There was little of equalitarianism in its development. There was much of pride in personal performance, and much self-consciousness; but an admiration for the magnate and a willingness to let him shine took the place of the jealous democracy of the Old West that resented visible signs of elevation or distinction.

Before the Civil War was over, the Middle West had become in a peculiar way the heart of the United States. As a section it had altered less from the standards of revolutionary and Jeffersonian democracy than had the other regions. Going its own gait, developing through repetition of the standard process farm by farm, it held true to type while the South was created as an entity with a civilization of its own, and the East was caught in new currents and deviated on a different course, and while the Far West arose to bar the extension of the West in perpetuity.

There is a constant temptation upon the historian who interests himself with the problems of the American frontier, to try to think along the lines of science and to find analogies to biological processes in the emergence of the social order of the West. There are points at which, as I have suggested some time back, the problem resembles that of the origin of species and the differentiation of types by selective breeding. The western was different from the eastern from the moment of his origin, and he persisted in the difference. How came he so; and why did he persist?

This focal question, I suppose, is one that is incapable of answer in our present light and may forever be unanswerable. Was the American a new social species, a fresh creation, and really different; or was he no more than the result of environment and selection that brought out human traits as old as Adam, retarded other traits primeval in their creation, and embodied only a new balance from the old stock?

But from the standpoint of the politician and the historian the question is whether he is to deal with a new species that will persist, or merely with a new variety, produced by crossing and selection, that may return to type once the special conditions cease to operate. There is of course a third possibility, that because of environment new characteristics have appeared in an old species. But our scientific friends tell us that acquired characteristics cannot stick, and so long as they are emphatic on this point the historian may raise the point, but he may not presume to answer it.

When next we meet, I shall do what I can to bring out the facts that bear upon the question whether the West will vanish when the conditions that accompanied its appearance go. There is time tonight, I think, to consider a little further the environment that seems to have made the initial imprint upon the Middle West, and to have kept it fairly true to type while the other regions of the United States have yielded to new influences and their resulting trends.

We have already seen a good deal of the uniformities of type, and the uniformities of condition that prevailed along the border, when the West was new. Our American pioneers were so much alike in age, in wealth, in ambition, that they possessed a promise of greater solidarity than prevailed in any of the communities from which they came. They had a suggestion of religious solidarity too. The church of Rome and the church of England were notably absent from the group of religions that met the frontier needs. In few parts of the United States was the Catholic church of dominant importance until a long time after the Great Migration, and until it spread its communions to serve the newer racial groups. It was to become one of the elements in the differentiation of East from West as time went on; but throughout the generation of Clay and the American System it was only one of the minor forces of the West. The Episcopal church was of greater force in the United States than the Catholic, but its communicants were never more than a scant minority among the people of the cabins. Its hold was on the wealthier classes of the East, whose contribution to the western procession was less important than that of most of the other single groups.

The religious currents that flowed most freely through the West were protestant and dissenter; and as the frontier shifted from the Appalachian Valleys to the Mississippi they experienced a change that is marked by a transition from the hard theology of the Presbyterian to the emotion of the Methodist. In the earlier phases of the frontier life there was little organized religion of any faith, but the craving of the Scotch-Irish who dominated the Old West for their Presbyterian church gave a Presbyterian color that still remains in that vicinity. But the craving was not capable of universal satisfaction, for no source of educated parsons existed in the United States until Princeton College took its shape; and it was never possible to make the parsons as rapidly as the congregations used them up. On the border the longing for re-

ligion was a real emotion, and the same forces
that dropped the qualifications for the elector
and the office holder, made the western citizen
more anxious for services of the spirit than he
was particular about its brand of sect.   The
Great Revival at the opening of the last century carried itself away from the possibility of
control by any highly organic church.   Local
and personal sects were multiplied.   Men with
a message built up congregations of their own,
and religion with a passionate emotion carried
more widely than creeds with an articulated
theology.   None of the denominations met the
frontier requirements more fully than did the
Methodists and the Baptists; and the prevalence
of these gives to the frontier of the Great Migration, that became our Middle West, an additional solidarity, remnants of which are still
more than visible to the naked eye.

The similarities of occupation prolonged the
duration of the similarities of type.   The vital
problems of the cabineer, up to the moment
when his firstborn child was ready to flit the
cabin, were filled with dull monotony and cease-
less labour.   And what he was doing from dawn
till candle-light, and from spring to fall, was
being repeated with trifling variation over the
whole region in whose creation he was taking
part.   There was a standardization of thought

that could not have been escaped. And so long as there remained a farming border, on which the essential processes could be repeated, the whole of the region of the Middle West was subject to continuous re-infection by the frontier spirit, with virus freshly reproduced by the cultures of the cabin life.

It should be noted that after the sharp differentiation of the four American sections we have had under observation—the East, with a western margin in a line not far from Pittsburgh; the South with a northern margin somewhat above the line of cotton culture; the Far West, with eastern demarcation at the edge of the zone of precious metals; and the Middle West—only the Middle West had a fresh geographic area into which to grow. In the other three, East, South, and Far West, there was room for greater intensification of effort, and for growing density of population, but none of them possessed an untouched area wherein could be repeated far into the future the processes of loneliness and isolation, and of primeval struggle in the conversion of virgin soil to farms. The Middle West had this. From its boundary of the period of the Civil War, which was not far beyond Omaha and Kansas City, to an uncertain point far up the plains where lack of rainfall blocked the farther penetration of the

farm, lay an area for another farming empire.
From north to south this zone stretched from
the Canadian boundary until somewhere in Okla-
homa it turned to cotton country.   Into this
region, bounded by South, Far West, and Middle West, only the Middle West as such could
penetrate.   We shall take another longer look at
this last American frontier when next we meet.
For our present purpose we may merely note
that for a long time after the other three of our
American regions reached a stage of equilibrium
the Middle West continued able to reproduce itself.   To unity of stock, and similarity of job,
this adds long life and repetition that induced a
settled habit.

But there was more to the Middle West than
these factors that I have tried to sketch.   There
was, for the region of the Great Migration, an
essential unity in geographical set-up that was
even more compelling than the unities of the
Appalachian Valley that in our earlier period
brought into the American colonies a community
of purpose lacking before they pushed from the
coastal plain to the piedmont and the mountains.
This set of unities began with the routes by
which the Middle West was reached; it was continued by the one-ness of outlet for the western
produce; it was consolidated by the similarity of
agricultural conditions that, from Cincinnati to

St. Paul and from Cleveland to Topeka, made
the small farmer the standard type of producing
citizen.

The migrants of the Great Migration, moving
from the Appalachian Valley into the Middle
West, did not advance along a broad and even
front. They were forced to pick their way; and
nature which fixed the gaps through which they
entered the great valley had fixed other gaps
along the western rim through which they might
emerge. The blending process whose tendency
was to produce a standard mixture among the
Americans of the valleys was carried one step
farther as the children of these Americans
thronged the three or four main roads that led
them down the approaches to the Mississippi
Valley. The upper Tennessee, the Cumberland, and the Kanawha carried their share of
the Great Migration without at any time rival-
ling the greatest of the routes, the Ohio River
itself. Mobilizing on the Monongahela and the
Youghiogheny, floating down these devious
streams to the Ohio in arks and flats and scows,
with family and livestock and household goods
stowed in meagre space, the great human stream
poured along the southern boundary of the
northwest States. Where the water took them,
they went. In a roadless land, they turned
away from the watercourses reluctantly and with

greatest difficulty.   And as they moved to their
new locations in the older States of Kentucky
and Tennessee, and to the newer ones of Ohio,
Indiana, Illinois, and Missouri they were conscious all the time that the natural course of the
current turned their faces away from home, and
toward the Mississippi.

The effect of the Mississippi in inducing a
social one-ness throughout its basin, resembles
in a certain way that of the Nile in bringing
to Egypt an early national government.
Whether they would or not, the river controlled the habit of life.   The Nile, indeed,
dominated agriculture with its irrigation
ditches as well as its traffic.   The Ohio, and its
Mississippi continuance to New Orleans, dominated traffic.   Before Clay formulated his
American System to cure the traffic ills and
marketing problems of the Middle West, the
Mississippi provided almost the only hope of a
market.   At every stage of national history we
may see the Mississippi bringing a unity of purpose to the West, and by indirection causing the
Federal Government to become more national in
the attempt to ward off the dangers of a western secession precipitated by the commercial interest.   We are not here much interested in the
reactions of the West upon the East, but we are
much concerned by the effect of topography in

holding the inhabitants to a closer unity of purpose than they might have had.

The dominance of the Mississippi in western trade continued until the Civil War. The internal improvements of Henry Clay were slow in coming, the Federal Government gave reluctant aid, private capital was scarce and cautious. The railroad movement which was finally to substitute an artificial channel for the one of nature did not become a reality until Clay had lost his great concern for economics and had engaged in desperate struggle to keep slave labor from breaking down the Union. And the real effect of the railroad in freeing the West from the dominance of a single direction was not seen until the Civil War began.

The leaders of the Old South entered on their great adventure, knowing well the dependence of the West upon the Mississippi. They believed that destiny bound the upper valley permanently to themselves. They counted on the early secession of the Border States, and felt sure that on victory the position of most of the Northwest would be untenable in the Union, and that they might anticipate its union with themselves. But when their military effort closed the Mississippi, and cut away the market for the western staples the unanticipated happened. The railroads of the Old Northwest got themselves under the new load, and after a few months of congestion and flounder allowed the resources of the interior to flow east along the loyal routes to the Great Lakes and to New York. Perhaps no other circumstance did more to wreck the southern cause. The West would not secede, and the Border States were driven by self-interest to play the part of the neutral. We have before us today an imposing struggle to gain for New Orleans what secession threw away, the commerce of the Mississippi Valley. And even yet, a century and a quarter after James Wilkinson drew his Spanish pension, and Aaron Burr led the western leaders to an uncertain Mississippi Valley goal, the great river gives a unity to the section that has become the Middle West. From Pittsburgh on the Ohio to Bismarck on the upper Missouri, the extended arms of the Father of Waters gather the Middle West in a vast embrace that still has a meaning.

And between the arms that embrace or touch a dozen States there lies a farming region perhaps without a parallel for its huge extent, its temperate climate, its uniformity of soil and natural resource. So long as men must eat, and so long as synthesis does not produce our food, the deep rich soils will make the Middle Western farms endure. The man who farms them will continue to react to the conditions of his life.

There will be something in common for the farmer in Ohio and the farmer in Dakota, and the radio broadcaster from his Chicago cell will know that he has an audience of a quarter of the American people with a common outlook. He will know, as well, if he knows his history, that this outlook has a closer resemblance to that of Clay and Lincoln and Andrew Jackson, of Thomas Jefferson and George Washington, than is the outlook of any of the other three sections of the nation. He will not expect it always to be right; but he will know that if he votes against its settled conviction, he will do so at his risk. For it is still capable of unity of action, and clarity of vision. And in every section of the United States there still survive enough Americans who have retained what their sections as a whole have lost, and there still remain in all the groups enough vestiges of the native traits, to make it fairly sure that when this Middle West is dead in earnest the rest of the Union will contribute votes enough to create a typical majority that will determine national fate.

CHAPTER III

WHEN THE WEST HAS GONE

THE generation of the present, to which I
hope to direct your attention now, opens upon
an uncertain future; uncertain because it has
not yet occurred, and whatever lies behind the
curtain is unknown. The more uncertain because the standard forces that have compelled
our destiny have dropped from view, and there
is a break in our connection with the continuous
past.

The generation begins, for our immediate
purpose, on the Tuesday following the first
Monday in November, 1896, when another revolt
of western liberalism broke out in open battle.
The first of these revolts, as we have seen, was
a revolt against the English Tories with George
Washington, rebel and patriot, as its personification. A generation later Thomas Jefferson,
Democrat, marshalled the second western wave,
and installed his dynasty. Andrew Jackson,
next, with Democrats behind him, descended
from the West in 1828 to take the spoils from
the enemies of true Americanism. And a generation after Jackson came Abraham Lincoln,

like all the rest a personification of some of the aspects of human dignity and liberal thought.

Every generation had its wave, each had its prophet, each swept from west to east with a new message, and each left the whole United States somewhat more firmly set to democracy than it was before.

The conditions that isolate this date of 1896 as the critical moment of a new period are found in the fact that a generation after Lincoln another wave of liberal protest swept our borders, another messiah came with a message of hope for common men, another battle between the forces of the frontier and the East was staged; and then history ceased to repeat itself. McKinley was elected President of the United States, and William Jennings Bryan was blocked from access to the niche that might well have perpetuated his name and memory in the sequence that begins with Washington.

Something had happened to break the course of normal development of American thought and action. From the beginning of things until our election of 1896 the trend of American life had with never a pause developed uneasiness among the conditions of the open frontier. The uneasiness was in the habit of accumulating, with increasing tension, until the moment of revolt occurred, and the leader made his appearance.

The outbreak invariably upset the balance of our politics and installed new rulers. Four times in a century the process repeated itself, and the four leaders rank so well among the defenders of the faith and the leaders of humanity that no American can speak of any of them without a thrill of conscious pride. But now the sequence stopped. There has been no new and dominant political party since the Republicans appeared, the marginal protests have risen, roared, and been absorbed or died away. For more than three-score years and ten no presidential leader has ever taken over control of our destiny without first making his peace with the old organizations that direct our politics; and it appears that we have changed our style of life, if not its content.

The question that I would lay before you to-night arises as a natural result of the matters that we have considered in the past. Given an environment, and nature gave it us, in which the normal restrictions of society are relaxed and emphasis is founded upon the elements of personal strength, courage, and endurance; given in short the sort of frontier that we call the West, we see opened a new episode in human history and a new set of values for the common man. The American was more than a mere native of America. He was survivor of a process of relentless selection; he was resultant of a new combination of economic and social forces. He was newer than he knew he was, and unconsciously he raised up a civilization that had in it something of a challenge and an ideal for the oppressed of all the world.

Given this; and next given a unit area persistent in its traits and tendencies; given the Mississippi Valley between the far-flung arms of its northern rivers; given a region from Pittsburgh to Kansas City and beyond, from Cincinnati to Omaha and Bismarck; given all these things, and for a century the American type repeats itself until it begins to look as though what might have been only a sport upon the social stock has become a species with peculiar habits of its own. And then we change the set-up; or nature does it for us. Free land gives out. We pass the margin of increasing returns. Industrialization catches up. The question then arises, and it is our question this evening, whether what we have is but an episode, a mere flash in the vast procession of humanity; or whether perchance it is a new beginning, with a permanent residue for human advantage and happiness.

The question is larger than the little interests of the United States. We are close to its centre, but upon the answer depends a whole philosophy; and we cannot give the answer yet. We can only guess, and look beneath the curtain of our future. But on the answer that humanity finally gets, the world must base its approach to future for all time. If the human race is full grown, and more is not to be expected of it; if the same old Adam is to repeat himself with only the variations that we are accustomed to, we may as well all of us give over and become behaviourist and opportunist, abandon humanity, and each get what he can. But if, on the other hand, something of human values shall persist, so that the American, lucky in his genesis, shall not only retain his luck but shall have a little left over for mankind; if by environment we may not only make the human immediately more comfortable but improve his offspring and their opportunity, then we shall be warranted in accepting an ideal of progress, in looking for a better world, and in making it worth the while of our best minds to expend their thought not upon individual advantage but upon schemes of construction. We may hope to relax the lines of caste, to stimulate the aspirations of the soul, and to bring to life a world in which mankind shall not be limited to what the Declaration of Independence calls "the pursuit of happiness," but shall in fact attain it.

As we approach this question that I pose, the

meaning that lifts our study of the frontier above the level of mere local history and curious antiquarianism, let us consider first the nature of that fifth successive revolt of western liberalism and inquire why it failed to repeat the process of our political genesis. Then let us examine the clash in America between that frontier force which is our unique contribution to civilization, and the set of world forces of accommodation to standard type. Then let us risk the dangers in gazing at the future. Shall we become merely a part of western civilization? Are we destined to behold an angry and despairing proletariat? Will our wealth operate differently from other wealth as it projects itself across our borders and takes up the tasks of world development that Europe used to dominate? Is progress only a concept of the poets and the immature, or has it some solid basis in the experience of our race? I have no notion that I can answer any of these questions, but it may be that in stating them we may see somewhat more clearly the limitations that they imply, and be a little clearer in our minds and souls as we and our people face the future, now that our West is gone.

The Populist revolt that reached its crest in 1896 has suffered in the judgment of posterity as all revolts must suffer when they fail to pass that mystic line that separates impractical from practical, wrong from right, treason from patriotism. It failed of its intent to drive into the discard one of the two major parties. It never gained control of the Government of the United States. Its history has been written by its enemies and in the light of its unsuccess. Yet as a movement in American thought and politics it so closely resembles the western movements that preceded it that in its final placement it must stand or fall with them. Not all of its measures can pass the test of critical judgment; but each of our great and useful waves of thought and feeling has been packed with nonsense as well as truth, and the men who sweated in the fight have generally been unable to discriminate between them. The essential elements in each of the political revolts have been their origin in and connection with a new frontier, their assumption that the immediate need of the West must be the panacea for the nation, and the residue of liberalism in each that has kept the West West, and has prodded the rest of the Union to a livelier preservation of its American traits.

Populism had its roots in the new frontier that developed alongside the Middle West when the railroads opened up what had been the old so-called desert, and when farmer homes pushed up the plains and encroached too hopefully upon the arid slopes where farming ceases to be an occupation and becomes a hazardous game of chance. At our last meeting we saw the four sections that by 1865 had come to comprise the Union. The East, the South, and the Far West contained, each of them, something at variance with what had been our original Americanism and had become the West and then the Middle West. The last American frontier lay between the Missouri River and the Rocky Mountains, and was adjacent to the Middle West. The people who reclaimed it came in varying measures from each of the four older sections. They came as well from northern Europe and added more alien bloods than the frontier mixtures had yet known. Böjer and Rölvaag and Hamlin Garland have saved us something of their spirit as they spread the genius of the middle border upon the plains, and fought with the giants of the earth while they carved out their homes. Year by year the zones of farms projected the Middle West upon the plains; and year by year, as had been the course of events since the beginning, the problems of the pioneers sought happy solutions, and brought out great movements. The spirit of the Far West did not perpetuate itself upon this last American frontier, nor the spirit of the South, nor that of the

East. It was the West that broke the sod and
made the farms until the last free land was gone
and the frontier episode reached its end.

The common qualities of land, and credit,
and markets, make this last of the Wests like
all its predecessors in many of its primary reactions. It was national in its aspirations, it was
debtor in its psychology, it was still searching
for a market that would make it solvent and
continue it in independence. There was nothing
new in these.

The novelty in its set-up is to be found in the
modern accompaniments that presided at its
birth. It knew the railroad. Between the ancient pioneer and his former home lay a trail,
long and hard, and dominated by adverse nature. Between the pioneer on this last trek and
his former home lay no mere force of nature but
a thing of man, a mechanical device, owned by
distant wealth, controlled by a bloodless corporation that was in its turn owned by absentees
who knew little of their property. The railroad
and the corporation were scapegoats on this last
frontier when times were bad. They impinged
upon the interest of every citizen, they took toll
as they brought him to his farm, as they carried
away his wheat, as they brought him the coffin
in which he was to be buried. They were inevitable and they were soulless. They were uni-

versal, and no man could avoid their contacts. They gave direction to feeling and intellect. The destructive forces of frontier thought were turned loose upon them as agents of inhumanity and greed. The constructive forces sought for means to control by law these institutions of service so that they might aid rather than devour. No one who has studied the history of railroads in the West can escape the conviction that the frontier had its grievance, genuine and profound; nor can he avoid a recognition of the fact that the grievance grew by being brooded over, and that the convenient scapegoat was forced to carry the odium of sins that were not his.

The last frontier knew the railroad; and it needed wealth. We have seen a little of the outlay of capital that was the price of settlement at any place or any time. The Granger farmer, or the Populist farmer, needed all the capital that any of his fore-runners required; and then he needed more. The physical and material standards of living were rising, and he desired to acquire them. Machinery had been invented for the farm. He needed his reaper and his thresher. The pioneer of the Great Migration, like the pioneer of the Appalachian Valley, could make for himself most of the tools of his ancient craft; or if he lacked technique

the local blacksmith could render all the assistance he desired.   But Cyrus H. McCormick de-
vised his reaper, and machinery thereafter multiplied the output of the farmer.   It cost money,
and increased the thickness of the blanket of
debt that every frontier incurred.   Debtor reactions, and antipathy to creditors when times
were hard grew with the burden of the frontier
debt.   It was no novelty for debtor farmers to
think it honest to save themselves by monetary
panaceas.   Daniel Shays had thought as much,
and his gangs of farmers demanded paper
money.   The relief statesmen of Kentucky had
thought as much, and banks of the commonwealths had been created to lend their notes to
voters on the basis of the borrower's need rather
than that of his collateral.   The Greenbackers
had developed the grand notion, grand to them,
of paying off the debt of the Civil War by the
easy process of the printing press.   All frontier
regions grow because they can get into debt,
and most of them have found the unromantic
process of paying off the debt a source of pain.
The debtor psychology and inflation movements
seem to be linked inseparably.   And this last
frontier of ours was subject to all of the com-
plexes that any frontier had known, speeded up
by the rapidity of steam, made heavier by the
greater need of capital.

The crystallization of these raw materials of protest politics occurred when the spread of occupation used up all of the land, and more of it, than could be farmed by traditional farming methods; and when a decade of hectic speculation in industry as well as farming had tied up all our fluid wealth; and when the vagaries of climate brought a halt to continued farming on the higher plains. It was intensified by the fact that, about the same moment, the cotton farmer had at last supplied his market. For three quarters of a century the cotton planter throve in spite of wasteful labor and destructive farming. The market for textiles grew faster than his costs. But in the decade that preceded Bryan the spindles of the cotton mills began for the first time to run more yarn than the world required. The opening of fresh cotton lands brought ruinous competition to the older plantations. The episode of cotton finished one chapter and entered on another, and panic that was general and painful in the whole United States was murderous along the border and in the South.

Populism was a crystallization of the elements of discontent, an accumulation of remedies for farmers who could not meet their debts, a new view of the relations of the common man who now with vision sharpened if not clarified by hunger saw a necessity in controlling wealth and its corporate agents so that they might serve democracy, not direct it. In the world outside, the philosophies of socialism and anarchy were being heard and tested. The United States saw in the rising institutions of industrialism a challenge to democracy. And once more, and true to form, it was a West that formulated new demands.

Step by step the unorganized grievances of the West were reduced to words, to platforms and to programs.

No historian has yet given an adequate portrayal of the similarities of step and method by which this process of translating western feelings into concrete politics has five times been enacted. The first carrier of the grievance of the high plains was the Farmers' Alliance whose network of organization spread rapidly over the disaffected area before 1890. The name of People's Party came only after there was a real basis in organization; and in 1892 there were national candidates launched in the presidential election. Many of the older of the leaders of this new people's cause had thirty years or so before been among the organizers of the Republican Party, and they were continually cheering their followers by pointing to the moderate beginnings of the anti-Kansas-Nebraska men in 1854, the Frémont Campaign of 1856, and the victory in 1860. To these, 1892 was the trial heat, and 1896 was to be the final race. They looked to history to repeat itself, and they accepted recruits in the crusade against the two old parties wherever they could be found, and whatever the motive of the revolt. It was an accident rather than an essential that the remedy for the debtor farmer was elevated to the first of the reforms demanded. This remedy in free-silver struck so definitely at fair play, class interest, and national good faith that the older parties played it up beyond its real deserts. The eastern opposition made Populism look like nothing but a movement of repudiation and inflation, and once it was so branded it could never shake off the reputation.

Bryan did not even want to shake it off. In the mind of William Jennings Bryan free silver was at once a proper remedy, and a symbol of the rights of the common people against the encroachment of entrenched wealth. His great oration before the Democratic convention in Chicago in 1896 brought results beyond those of most orations. It made him the candidate of the party, and it impressed the thoughtless as a *tour de force* of oratorical genius. But it was not *tour de force*. He had been making the speech, repeating the parts in varying combina-

tions, for at least five years. Never had he had
so significant an audience, or so immediate returns. But there was nothing new in it or
unusual in him. There were dozens of minor
politicians performing, with what earnestness
and intelligence they had, the part of the advo-
cate of the new western cause.

It was highly appropriate that the Populist cause should be so widely spontaneous and
so often anonymous. The common man was
more nearly carrying on his own revolt than he
had done before. No single leader brought him
to the battle. But Bryan was a true symbol of
a movement one of whose convictions was that
the known leaders of both old parties had be-
trayed their groups, and that the people must
serve themselves if they were to be served at all.

Nothing is abnormal about the Populist revolt, except its end. It lost. It failed to repeat
a process of success that had been so often repeated that it might almost be assumed. More
than this, the date of Bryan's defeat separates
a period in which new issues have made new
parties, one by one, from a period in which no
new party of consequence has come from any
source; and there has been no new issue upon
identification with which any great party has
been willing to risk its future. The United
States has not ceased to get results, but the

process has changed, and no one now expects to
see repeated the old method of advance by
reiterated western thrusts.

Bryan's defeat opens a period in which the
American historian is only just beginning to
feel his way around. It has not ended. The
end is not even in sight. We approach the
period lacking the convenient thread of growth
that improves the unity of the hundred years
preceding it. But the open frontier is gone;
that hardy constant of the American past has
disappeared. A wave of genuine frontier emotion has been resisted; and our history ceases to
repeat itself. We are confronted with a demand
to know why Bryan was stopped, and what it
was that stopped him.

It was not, I think, the personal magnetism
or the political repute of William McKinley
that defeated Bryan and the western process.
These were great, but not sufficient. There
were included among McKinley's Republican
supporters many who would have preferred another on the ticket, for they doubted his willingness to take punishment or stand without yield-
ing in the face of possible defeat. They
doubted his soundness upon the money question
that was major issue of the canvass. And there
was nothing about him that inspired enthusias-
tic loyalty and self-sacrifice to equal that with

which the youthful Bryan impregnated his followers.

Nor was it alone the organizing genius of Marcus Alonzo Hanna who directed the campaign as he had directed the candidacy of McKinley for the nomination. Hanna was shrewd and resourceful and devoted to both his party and his ticket. He knew how to raise money and where and when to spend it. He was indeed the business man in politics. But organization alone could not have withstood the outbreak of sentiment, passion, and local interest. There was something more than this that had come into the East and North to give it compactness and coherence. Hanna and McKinley were visible symbols of a spiritual and economic condition; but it was the condition rather than the symbols that offered the resistance and turned the tide.

The history of the United States is, from one point of view, a history of recurrent invasions. The colonial settlers constituted only the earliest of these; but they provided the human raw material upon which the succeeding invasions were to work, as well as the human raw material, changed by access to a frontier environment, that was to resist the invasions and modify their direction or their character. The later invasions are at various times invasions of men, of wealth, of institutions, and of ideas.

We know little as yet of the courses taken by the invasion of wealth that continued to flow almost until the opening .of the World War. Only now, as the second quarter of our century opens, are students turning seriously to what is described as economic imperialism; and so many of the students have their minds made up in advance that we are seeing evil consequences and unrestrained cupidity magnified to many times their diameters, without getting a fair picture of the way in which the wealth of those who had it has been employed by those who had it not in the task of making new quarters of the world habitable and productive. I have no brief tonight for either side of the argument upon the present status of economic penetration; but I should like to insist that without a study of the way in which the wealth of Europe was turned to use in America one can no more understand the causes of the American Revolution, or the economics of the plantation, than he can understand the financial vagaries of the wildest of our domestic frontiers. But this invasion of wealth is one whose significance has been lessened as Americans have accumulated capital of their own with which to replace the wealth that they have borrowed.

The invasions of men have had their ups and downs. The first of them laid the foundations of European civilization on the seaboard. The second, in the eighteenth century planted and entrenched the English power in the settlements of the Appalachians. The third, in the middle of the nineteenth century, played a mighty part in influencing that deviation that made of the East a section different from the American tradition. The fourth, which reached one crisis in the early eighties and another in our own times, provided the human materials on which to build an industrialism in imitation of that of Europe. And this industrialism itself is an invasion to which we must attribute much of the responsibility for the victory that Mc-Kinley led and Hanna marshaled.

For reasons that must be clear to one who has studied the frontier setting of so much of our American life, the industrial revolution came to American shores a good many years after it was flourishing in Europe. Here was little free capital for investment; and industry called for a large capital account. There was small incentive for Europe to advance the capital, for every American mill was a threat at the markets of the mills of Europe. There were few Americans anxious to take wage jobs, for frontier opportunity set them thinking in other ways. And so it was that the manufacturing cities of Europe were well along upon their modern course before the small beginnings were visible along the line of the New England water powers. The protective tariff, which was Clay's link to bring the East into the articulation of the nation that he conceived, rose into prominence as the manufactures themselves increased in number. Before the Civil War we may see throughout the East the promise of an industrial network, and some of the performance. There was enough of it to make more emphatic the differences that distinguish the East from the South or West. The effect of it was to solidify our politics and our party organization.

So far as our party organization is concerned, its history falls into two distinct periods depending upon whether parties existed chiefly to carry out ideas or to produce results. For nearly a century after independence the great questions of national controversy, upon which men divided, and for the advancement of which they associated themselves in parties, were largely matters of national or human theory. So far as the individual income of the citizen was concerned, it did not matter greatly who won. Few felt that a given election would either make or break. And men gave themselves more freely to the play of ideas in politics than could be

done after the advent of industrialism had made
the content and action of government more important than the political theories underlying
it.   The four western revolts, upon which in
turn Washington and Jefferson, Jackson and
Lincoln were brought into power, were not without a mixture of self-interest and class greed,
but they had a high theoretical content and a
low percentage of supporters whose assistance
was founded upon a hope of gain.

But before Bryan led the fifth revolt into
battle the industrial tendencies had reached a
point at which new allies appeared to give to
party theory the cement of personal advantage.
The protective tariff grew to a stature which
Henry Clay had never conceived.   Between
1880 and 1892 it had become clear to nearly
every American who manufactured goods, to
those whose incomes were derived from industry,
and to those whose wages depended upon the
steady operation of the mills, that Republican
success might mean prosperity while Democratic victory might well be the prelude to
panic.   Even today it is difficult for a Republican orator to discuss the tariff without arguing
that the disastrous panic of 1893 was induced
by a fear of Democratic tariff of 1894.   Collec-
tors of the Republican campaign funds told the
great industrialists that their contributions

were an insurance of prosperity, and figured out for them what they might lose should "tariff for revenue only" become the basis of tariff legislation. No Populist orator could show to his followers that a personal gain on such a scale would follow victory; and his audiences had so little that they had nothing to lose after a defeat. Here was a factor that gave to both the old parties sinews of war with which to fight the insurgency of the Populist West, and to the Republican party of Hanna and McKinley it gave sinews, program, and a prospect of victory.

Not only had the tariff given elements of power to the older parties before 1896, but the whole tendency of the chief panacea of the Populists was to increase those elements. Free silver, and the other measures of inflation that inspired the Populists with hope, inspired a panic of equal intensity among the classes and in the regions that the Populists opposed. Wherever there was capital in the United States there was a fear of the loss to be occasioned by free silver and the fifty-cent dollar. It was no stage battle. It was panic bred by a fear of repudiation and confiscation. When in the last weeks of the canvass of 1896 it looked as though the cause of the silver-tongued orator of the Platte might win, the Republican field-marshal,

Hanna, went to lower New York, and from the banks and the insurance companies, from the custodians of the resources of industrial society, gathered campaign funds to avert defeat.   I have no interest in any of the suggestions of corruption in the use of this money at the polls. It costs money, much money, to bring an idea to the people.   But from the standpoint of party perpetuity alone, quite distinct from the soundness of party theories, the course of the industrial process had created in the East classes with an accumulated wealth that they might use, and with an expectation that personal advantage was connected with party victory.

Party organization, in our earlier style, lacked the cement of economic hopes, and it was possible to overturn a party with a new idea. So long as frontier types were in the saddle, and so long as even the East was not far removed from the simplicity and debtor status of the West, and so long as the national Government was not expected to be the agent of prosperity, our parties rose and fell and the ideas that generated them were bred or grafted in the centres of border democracy.   By 1896 the open West was nearly all in use, and the fresh frontier had ceased to be.   The unique condition of our America experience had reached its end, and with its passing its derivatives were bound to fade. The other conditions—those which came to America with the industrial revolution, the accumulation of native wealth and the resultant urbanization of society—had by 1896 reached a state of readiness for pitched battle, and their victory over frontier politics marks the termination of an era.

In the United States of the future there is little hope, or fear, of a repetition of the political processes of the past. Since 1860 no new party has taken control. In 1896 an old party met and repelled a western wave. The new aims of government, and the bony structure of party organization, have kept the major parties alive and able both to survive defeat and to meet the disruptive forces of sectional insurgence. We have seen the gallant effort of Roosevelt to found a new party, and the ease with which the remnants of his Progressive group were absorbed back into the old organization. We have seen a LaFollette movement with a Farmer-Labor label, and this too we have watched in its phases of dispersion and re-absorption. New ideas have not ceased to invigorate old parties, or to gain majority authority and national enactment, but the old method that was repeated so often that it seemed almost to be a law of our nature, has ceased to operate.

The two great forces that have made the

United States today, thus stand out clearly against the background of our experience. The unique force, that of an open frontier with free land or cheap land for all, was an episode. While it lasted, from the time of the earliest establishments on tidewater until the grain farms of the Populists dried up on the high plains of western Kansas, it let loose the peculiar American contribution to human experience. But it lasted nearly three hundred years, and most of our history carries the record of the fertility of the frontier soil. The other force, that of accommodation to the environment of the western world, was rival to it, and to a degree is supplanting it. One may not say that it has defeated it. Until the frontier itself was gone, the frontier spirit carried the day. When McKinley won in 1896 his triumph was lessened by the fact that the frontier had lost the power and opportunity to perpetuate itself. Nothing can ever bring the frontier back. Our question for the future is not whether we may revive the simplicities and crudities of a pioneer civilization, but rather whether the residuum of our special history is to prevent a complete assimilation into the civilization of the western world or is merely to retard the extension of that civilization over the United States.

Our technique is changed, of course. As

we have seen, there is little reason to suppose that sectional points of view will create new party machines in the United States. But there is as little reason to believe that the going machines of party will continue to represent the same ideas unchanged from year to year. One has only to look at the history of the Populist program to realize the existence of a sort of political osmosis by which the basic principles of one party penetrate the hide of another, and receive enactment. The Populist Party, as such, went down in defeat. But in the ensuing twenty years, sometimes by Republican Congresses and sometimes by Democratic, the income tax and farm loans, the initiative and the referendum and corrupt practice legislation made perhaps a greater progress than they would have been likely to make under the guidance of victorious Populists themselves. It is a consequence of industrial development, and the rise of the public services, that our parties have acquired tough and articulated frames, strong enough to hold them together during the lean years of defeat. But it is a consequence of that federal growth whose inauguration we witnessed at our first meeting that a genuine emotion of interest, regardless of party, finds its way to our legislative chambers.

The influence of the old frontier was one of the liveliest of the forces that kept our thirteen States from holding on to an imperial control of an American empire. There were few precedents in history that suggested that the thirteen States could hold together in a federal compact at all. There were fewer precedents for any course of action by them except one of relentless and selfish administration of the common property, the western country, for their own advantage. It is part of the western story that the United States did the unexpected thing. The determination not to hold the open country as subject country but to use it for the creation of autonomous States, was a growth from a frontier germ. Its consequence is the United States of today, with its forty-eight still-separate States, and its federal structure at the top that still has barriers beyond which it does not operate. The genius of nineteenth century government was centralization, and then more centralization, with the unitary State as the objective. The structure of American experience did not entirely escape such tendency, but its design made it easier to hold back a general action; and at once harder for a dominant majority to control policy and easier for new ideas to get themselves launched, exposed to examination, and perhaps incorporated.

The recent experiment in North Dakota under the control of what has called itself a Nonpartisan League provides an illustration at this point. Here was a western agrarian movement, descended in its characteristics from Populism and all the liberal frontier reforms. Because of our distribution of powers, with the States still wielding large authority, it was a simple matter for the leaders of the local idea to gain local control and opportunity. In a normal centralized modern state, such logical heresies have little chance to get a hearing. Their spokesmen are laughed down or disregarded in the national assemblies. Even though the heresies should prove to be first phases of a new revelation they would have hard going.

But in the United States it is not hard to get a regional hearing, and the respectability that comes from local authority. In two years a local group may seize its State. In another two, if only it can continue to agree, it may amend the State constitution under the wide limits of the federal overhang, and change the basic law. It may begin to put spokesmen in the Congress within two years, and its Senators may follow close upon them. Whatever idea may manage to gain a local following may gain for itself a trial, with the eyes of all the United States upon the experiment. The consequences of an idea are thus limited to the people who accept it, until the period of experiment has passed. And the new idea, whether it be Populism or Nonpartisanry will either die easily within its local limits or spread because of its power to attract. The American federal scheme was not adopted because of its admirable qualities as an experimental social laboratory; but such it has become. And in a century sprinkled with revolutions and *coups d'état* in Europe the federal system seems to have operated as an American equivalent for revolution. The continuity of American administration has never wavered. The two parties have come to be crystalline and mechanical as parties. But they have learned to absorb and reflect new ideas that in the earlier period would have overturned them. In each of the parties you may find to-day men of every shade of opinion upon every issue before the people. Most of the more important legislation by the nation tends to become non-partisan in character. The parties flourish but ideas are enabled to prevail. And the American scheme of local autonomies provides easy testing grounds that most of our neighbours completely lack.

There is a real bearing of this upon the question whether we shall speedily be absorbed in the main currents of western civilization, or instead permanently remain a little different, because of our peculiar experience. If I may judge, the chief problems of the western world today are the relation between the industrial state and the proletariat that industry has created; the habit of accumulated capital to project itself in an imperial fashion; an increasing rigidity of life for the ordinary man, as he is held in the net of a complex society with no probable relief except through the agency of revolutionary socialism; and a waning of the old hope that the race is growing better and that regeneration is to be anticipated. Whether I am right or not in believing these to be the chief problems of the world today, they are at least important, and they invite our examination from the American angle of approach.

The American has been slow to learn the meaning of the word proletariat. The working classes of Europe had acquired definition many years before there was a considerable emergence of such a class in the United States. Karl Marx had launched his manifesto and had constructed his socialistic philosophy many years before Americans began to question the permanence of the freedom of opportunity that was the gift of the frontier. And not until the industrial element in American society was nearly ready to

hold its own against Bryanism did the nomen-
clature of industrial clash come to have any pre-
cise meaning in the United States.   Socialism
and communism, anarchy and nihilism, capi-
talism and economic determinism, seemed to re-
late to other worlds than ours until the eighties
of the last century.   Between the railroad strikes
of 1877 and the Pullman strike of 1894, an
American here and there came to know that the
words had meaning.   But still it seemed that
their meaning related to a sort of social disease
brought into the United States by the foreign
agitators whose own countries forced them into
exile.

The union movement, as a sympton of industrial society, came into American importance
during these years immediately before the clash
of Bryanism; but the growth of unionism failed
to follow the lines that Karl Marx predicted,
and today the status of the labour movement in
America is such as to warrant a belief that in
this side of our life the future will not bring an
identity with western Europe.   Apparently the
freedom of opportunity that prevailed so generally during the formative years of the American labour movement changed its direction and
character, so that the majority movements of
American labour have been a disappointment to

the leaders of the extreme left and to the advo-
cates of labour as a proletarian entity with a
mission to dominate the state.

It is not merely a matter of the degree to
which labour has been solidified in Europe and
in the United States; it is a matter of its spirit.
The Marxian prediction has more nearly been
fulfilled in Europe than in the United States.
There the last century has seen the rise of labour parties and the attempt to dominate the
states in the interest of the working class. The
bolshevist revolution represents merely the extreme development of labour's effort to dictate.
But in the United States labour as a whole has
declined to believe that it is fundamentally and
forever at variance with capital. The lines between have failed to stiffen. It has become more
difficult for the worker in the mills to become
director of the trust than it was for the barefoot
boy to pass through the cabin to social independence; but hope has remained, and there is
still enough reality to give it body. Labour has
seen its aims more in a bargaining for advantage than in an overturn of systems. Again
and again for fifty years the leaders of labour's
left wing have tried in vain to impregnate the
whole body with their revolutionary view of
labour's mission. The rank and file have remained American first, and workmen after-

wards. If not they, perhaps their children, might hope to get ahead. Instead of tearing down the ruling classes and the economic structure, they have voted billions into schools and have cherished the old hope of individual rise and social progress.

It is impossible for me to believe that this difference between American labour and that of continental Europe is not fundamental and permanent, or that it is not a derivative of the frontier experience that injected hope into our society more generally than had ever been possible among the common people of the races from whom we have sprung. While the frontier itself lasted as a reality there was almost no labour class among us, for opportunity and individual freedom were too widespread to admit of the development of an oppressed and restricted class of citizens.

And now that the frontier has gone I see no prospect of an embattled proletariat on this side of the Atlantic. There will be left-wingers and revolutionists; there will be plenty of occasion for nervous conservatives to fear the advance of inconvenient ideas. But without repressions there can hardly be explosions. For many generations to come, the leaders of labour will graduate to become the directors of productive capital, and labour will lack the leadership that comes from a rebellious and baffled general staff. The political structure, as we have seen, is such, that in so far as any group can attract votes it is at liberty to take possession piecemeal of our local governments, and to face the sobering experience of trying to convert theory into practice. It is the effective power of resistance of entrenched minorities that has turned most revolutions from evolutions into cataclysms, and that has converted the workers into "wage-slaves" and the working classes into destructive proletariats. The frontier influence that retarded the emergence of a working class, placed hope where hope had rarely been before; and it advanced a decentralized organization that leaves our local units easy of control by any new movement that is strong enough to command respect. The word proletariat is likely long to remain an unusual word in the mouth of the American, and to derive most of its meaning from a society whose history is different from ours.

If I am right at all in this, and if class warfare is not to be an imminent American diversion; if the American workers are to continue to believe that their partnership in the state is more important than their membership in an oppressed class; then there arises the question of how we may be expected to behave in the face of

the momentous fact that the working wealth of
the world is not evenly distributed. In all communities some have more and some have less;
and in a democratic community the minority
who have and direct the more do so only by the
tacit or expressed permission of the vast majority who have the less. In all nations there is
uneven concentration of the control of wealth.
The cities and the industrial districts do the
bulk of the financing, and the great agricultural areas depend for their working capital
and for their development or economic exploitation upon the centres of finance. And in the
set-up of world economics we have the so-called
backward regions, lacking the accumulated
wealth with which to develop their own resources, and the industrial regions with money
to invest.

I suppose that there is no more significant
matter before the world today than the manner
in which society shall project upon an international stage that old and baffling relationship
between him who has and him who lacks; between creditor and debtor. There is nothing
new in the fundamentals of the relationship.
The novelty is chiefly in the scale of its extension, and in the fact that the spirit of nationalism has to be faced, and the resulting clash of
jurisdictions. Shylock has always been a mem-

ber of the cast of the social drama, always essential and always unpopular. And now that he has been generalized under the imposing names of industrial imperialism and economic penetration, he looks bigger and more menacing than he really is, and his new names deceive the thoughtless into a belief that he himself is new.

We are not at this moment concerned with the basic problems of this economic imperialism; our duties are only with its relationship to the United States, and to the effect upon it of the organization we have derived from our frontier spirit and of the state of mind that persists now that the frontier is gone. The duality of our experience seems greatly to affect the picture at this point. The clash between the frontier forces and those of accommodation to world conditions has not progressed completely enough to form either a smooth and uniform mixture, or a chemical union in a new political balance. Instead, we are unpredictable at any single minute, or upon any particular application of principle to action. Senator Borah is capable of being at one time a sturdy irreconcilable upon matters of world reorganization and a believer in the possibility of an outlawry of war. And Senator Borah is an honest man.

We, as a people, are capable of being carried away by the notion of a super-state, modeled on lines like those of our federal government, and powerful enough to control the causes of war and to repress its practice. We showed this in 1918, with men as diverse as Woodrow Wilson and William Howard Taft on the same platform. But we are quite as capable of turning our back upon the world, letting it fry in its own fat, and exploiting a sort of lone-hand nationalism that is suspicious of every motive and rejects co-operation. This is proved in 1919 by the wide approval that accompanied our rejection of the Treaty of Versailles. It is no wonder that foreign statesmen are bewildered by American behaviour, or that since the rejection of the treaty we have received, as we still receive, a procession of curious European observers who are searching for some principle of action with which to explain the vagaries of American practice.

The answer is, I think, that we have not settled down to any pattern. One day or year we act as the children of pioneer fathers might be expected to act; the next we behave like wealthy owners of a share of industrial society. We shall I suppose eventually average up to a uniform policy. What will this policy have to say upon the subject of the projection of creditor influence across the lines of nationality, that we now call economic imperialism or penetration?

One of the influences upon American behaviour at this point may well be traced to our habit of assuming a superior authority with a right to judge. We scold often enough at the decisions of our courts, and of the supreme courts of state and nation that determine the validity not alone of causes but of laws themselves. But we are uniformly cool about it when our personal interest is not involved, and others scold. It is too much to hope, in this human world, that the loser of a suit shall ever pay tribute to the adequacy of the court. But there is an interesting possible contribution to a world order in this habit to which we have been bred. Even the colonies knew the power of review and rejection that vested in Parliament and the English courts. Our constitution gave to the Supreme Court jurisdiction over all cases arising under the constitution and the laws; and as the States have increased in number the assumption has become more and more complete that somewhere there needs to be a power capable of judging the acts of government and of reconciling them with the common and accepted principles of action.

The American mind, filled with the American habit of law, has no difficulty in comprehending a world order with a world court. Nationality and temporary views of local interest stand in the way of immediate acceptance of the particular world court that is offered. But when the moment comes at which it shall appear advantageous to attach ourselves, there will be no American habit of mind or action to be overcome. From our very beginnings of diplomacy we have led the world in advocacy and application of judicial methods of settling international disputes. Our type of government which has made it possible for New York and Iowa and California to remain reasonably happy under a single roof, to enjoy autonomy where it is needed and national rules where they are desired, has been largely the consequence of the pioneer requirements, and leaves us capable, at least, of coming to a future balance of opinion in which a genuine internationalism shall be outstanding. It would have been impossible for many Americans in the generation of Henry Clay to conceive a government of the United States that interfered with private business, with general approval behind it. But it took only fifty years for need to change, and opinion with it, so that before the century ended Congress took over a supervision of the common carriers and laid down a law upon the trusts. Who can tell when the fact of world-flung industry

will take hold of the American mind, and make
the United States a leader instead of a drag in
the movement for its judicial control?

The state of mind that we have inherited
from the experiences of the frontier period has
implications and suggestions for the future
quite as definite as are the precedents provided
by the American organization. We know much
from our own experience about the effect of
debt, and the way in which the debtor-creditor
relationship becomes a dangerous force when
the debtors are spread over one geographic area
and the creditors are concentrated in another.
One thing that the frontier contributed to the
American mind was an instinctive feeling that
the creditor was always selfish and generally
wicked. The long distance between them, as
eastern wealth was advanced for the development of western communities, added the element of absenteeism to make the matter worse.
But this matter of economic imperialism that
fills the world stage today is an old story in the
United States.

Our Atlantic frontier was a projection of
European economic influence in the century and
a half before the Revolution; and more of the
motives of that Revolution than we like to believe came from a willingness of colonial mer-

chants and planters to escape some of the obligations to their English creditors.

Our Appalachian frontier was again an economic projection from the older East, and a high proportion of its people carried with them to their mountain cabins a debt to the eastern regions that financed them. Among the difficulties in the adoption of the federal constitution was a fear that it would create new and powerful agencies that would increase the burden of the debts; and the makers of the frame thought it a sound protection to include provisions against the impairing of contracts and the issuance by the States of paper money.

The East again financed the Great Migration into the Ohio and Mississippi Valleys; and when the boom broke after the panic of 1819 there was hardly a western state that failed to take some step to protect the debtor against the rapacity of the creditor. It was easy to convince a frontier electorate that all creditors, remote and rich, were grasping, and that the debtors were victims of greed rather than speculative and improvident. Sometimes they were; but the significant thing was the deepening conviction along the border that the powers of capital were diabolic. And Andrew Jackson threw the driving power of his personality against the incorporation of the money power in the second bank.

Every frontier has begun on borrowed money and has passed through a period of relationship to eastern wealth that has a close resemblance to the relationship of Mesopotamia to Britain, of northern Africa to France, of Central America to the United States. It was economic projection from the start, and might as well always have been called penetration or imperialism if the frontier leaders had known the words. It produced sectional clash, the bank war, the Greenback movement, the free silver crusade. It diabolized Wall Street and has given anthropomorphic shape to the modern money trust. But it has been concealed because all of it happened within the bounds of a single nation, and most of its specific controversies could finally be reduced to legal causes that might come before a common court. If free silver had been a debtor-creditor clash between the Balkan States and France or between the United States and the war associates who owe us money, it might have contained the seeds of destructive wars. But the federal frame was inclusive enough to contain it all within itself, and flexible enough to absorb the shock.

There is an incongruity that has as yet received little attention in the present status of the United States. It has become a world creditor. In this capacity nature requires it to act as creditors must act. It feels the urge to collect the war debts, to protect American capital when it goes beyond our bounds, to set up quaint and irregular financial dictatorships among our weaker neighbours with the double purpose of lessening the danger of foreign interference and of assuring to American investors the produce of their investments. And yet the machine that does these things is a machine that owes what we have seen to a frontier past, and that is continually overwhelmed by survivals of a frontier spirit that has an instinctive belief that the creditor is generally wrong. No other nation than the United States could today, I think, have a considerable opinion that it ought not to try to collect debts due itself. Yet many and important Americans believe that the war debts ought to be forgiven. In this I suggest that they are acting in a frontier manner. No other nation seriously questions the propriety of protecting its nationals overseas, of taking steps to secure their investments, of gaining exclusive privileges for its citizens and taking pride in their advantage. The contradictions in the American behaviour are added to by the fact that this side of our experience makes it possible for Americans at once to denounce European imperialism and to defend their own; to attack their government when it protects its wealth and fosters economic penetration through dollar diplomacy, and in the same breath to insist upon a complete and self-sustained nationalism that denies any agency beyond that of national force for the maintenance of international justice.

The alternatives before the United States today, in our generation from which the actual frontier has gone but in which the spirit of the frontier has continued to survive, show themselves in these two vast fields that I have so briefly considered. Shall we fall in step with Europe, and develop a proletariat insistent upon control, or are we to continue with that openness of interest and chance that makes citizenship superior to class? The prospects of the latter seem to me greater than those of the former; and if we shall indeed avoid class warfare in a happy nation, I cannot escape the conclusion that we shall owe it chiefly to the happy consequences of our frontier life. Shall we, in the foreign field, develop our nationality, take advantage of our growing wealth, and become the world menace of the next century,— for no imperial power has ever stopped itself thus far; or are we capable of transferring our federal habit to a wider stage and of resuming a leadership whose conscious goal shall be the reduction of national ambitions, including our own, to a reign of reasonable law, interpreted by honourable courts, directed and controlled by a spirit of democratic life? The answer here is less clear to me than in the realm of our domestic clash of interests, but I am disposed to believe that such a development is not impossible. There would not have been any League of Nations today but for the leadership of an American president with American forces of international idealism behind him. We are capable of a repetition of the drive,—more capable than not; and when the new occasion shall come it may be that the executive himself may be more flexible, or may be freed from the terrible handicap of being a Democrat. And we may find ourselves giving strength and drive and continuity to an international experiment upon a larger scale.

I move with hesitation into this field of prophecy, and none need follow me. I may be wrong in my conviction that we are to escape class warfare as a consequence of the spread of industrial order. I may be unduly hopeful in suspecting that if the United States can continue to elevate citizenship above class-interest its example will have a tendency to disprove the inevitableness of class antagonisms, and will offer a different and more wholesome ideal than those of Marx, Lenin, and Mussolini. I cannot believe that democracy is done for, or that on the whole there is any superior foundation for government and the social order than that of the common people who live within them.

I may be wrong as well in imagining that the world can work out a federal order, with a fair balance between the principles of autonomy and uniformity; or that our nationalist United States may yet come cheerfully to accept a limitation of that nationality as it becomes absorbed within a federation of the world. Yet I believe that this too is something more than barely possible. And in both cases my confidence is grounded upon testimony that seems to me to be derived from an examination of our frontier past.

And should the historian of another generation test my guess, and be able to confirm it by the facts, where would we stand with reference to that old idea of progress? Is it a law of social organization seeking to free itself from impediments and impurities in order to operate; or is progress only will-o'-the-wisp that attracts light minds, and diverts them from the realities of life? Should my first two guesses stand the test of time, I should not greatly care. It makes little difference whether we be really happy or only think we are. If the American frontier should prove to be the happy episode in world experience that suggested the basis for a finer and truer co-operation within the nations and without, if it helped to bring about a world of justice built on law, the peoples who are still behind the curtain of the future would have the benefits that progress might have brought them, and would have no need to worry over ways and means.

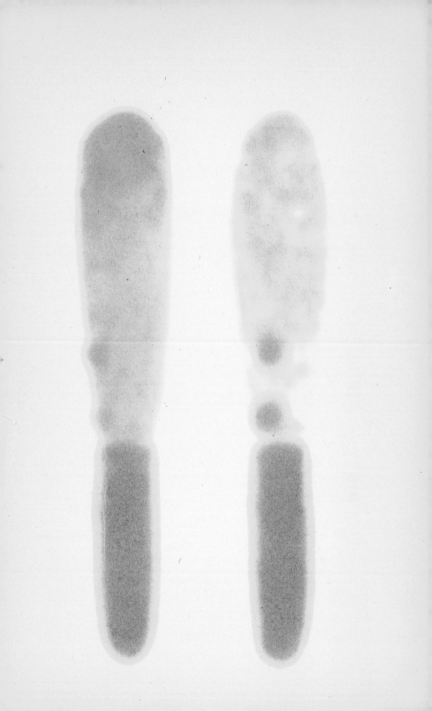

DATE DUE

GAYLORD   PRINTED IN U.S.A.